HARDPRESS.NET
HOME OF HARD-TO-FIND BOOKS

Fitful Fancies
by William Kennedy

Copyright © 2019 by HardPress

Address:
HardPress
8345 NW 66TH ST #2561
MIAMI FL 33166-2626
USA
Email: info@hardpress.net

386

FITFUL FANCIES,

BY

WILLIAM KENNEDY.

Φωνὴ βοῶντος ἐν τῇ ἐρήμῳ·

EDINBURGH;

PUBLISHED BY

OLIVER & BOYD, TWEEDDALE COURT;

AND

GEO. B. WHITTAKER, LONDON.

1827.

TO

THE RIGHT HONOURABLE

ROBERT PEEL,

THIS LITTLE BOOK

IS INSCRIBED WITH RESPECT,

BY

WILL. KENNEDY.

CONTENTS.

POÉMS.

SONGS.

NATIONAL SONGS.

POEMS.

POEMS.

THE SOLITARY.

In a sheltered nook, near a restless brook,
  Which freely speeds on its way,
Far remote from strife, I have made my life
  A perpetual holiday.
Green summer is gone, and brown autumn come,
  Since the world and I were twain,
Yet my worst and my only wish is, that
  We never prove one again.

In the farce of state, let them emulate
  The revelry of a king,
Who are only blest when a lofty crest
  Nods over their banquetting.

Much luck may they have of their sickly smiles,
    False hearts and poisonous fare !
But, freed from their touch, may the fiend me clutch
    When next I their pastimes share !

Dame Nature is good ; she hath given me food,
    To keep the wild spirit still ;
And hallows the night with slumberings light,
    And visions unmarred by ill.
And she fills the holiest cup on earth
    From the waters of the well,
Which, to suckle the new-born primroses,
    Through the rock's rude bosom swell.

In the days long sped I would fain have led
    A maid to the altar-stone ;
She smiled on me too, but I could not woo
    With wealth, so was left alone.
She wedded another who loved her not,
    And I lived, alas ! to see
Her beauty a waste, and her soul a wreck
    Of sin and of misery.

Then I vowed no more should my heart feel sore
   ' For a piece of varnished clay ;
And, in a deep mood of my solitude,
   I laboured both night and day,
Until a creation all faultlessness,
   Stood full in my fancy's view;
And to it I turn, in the hour of dreams,
   With devotion warm and true.

Here no faithful friend doth his counsel lend
   To strike roused Reflection pale,
As his tender breast makes the ear possessed
   Of some dark accusing tale :
Nor is one of the kind, acquainted crowd
   Ever seen to pass the door,
Where a treasure of loving and peaceful thoughts,
   Is its owner's only store.

But though man come not to this placid spot,
   There be choice society
Both in earth and air, that cheerfully share
   Their gladsome company.

In the joyous morn, from the cherry-tree
  Thrills the robin's piercing call ;
And they bid me hail, like a kindred thing,
  The wild-wood carollers all !

In the cloudless night, with the orbs of light,
  As they marvellously roll,
I hold converse strange, and the thought of change
  With deep hope fills my soul.
Then the pride of my wayward nature dies,
  I am as an infant meek,
And it seems not the breeze, but the hand of God
  Approving, that sooths my cheek.

I'll long bless the hour which gave me power
  The truth to value and know,
That a small measure of simple pleasure
  Is the rarest boon below.
Let him off to the world who thinks not so,
  And, when kneeling at its shrine,
With his heart's best hope obtained, let him ask,
  If his lot half equals mine.

EARTH AND THE SERAPH.

'Twixt orbs of the banned and spheres of the blest,
A Seraph had taken her airy rest ;
She heard a strange whisper of mourning and mirth,
And asked whence it came of the wandering Earth ?
" At an angel's summons I may not pause,—
Pierce through my cloud-robe and know the cause :
          Man's a stern Hunter !"

The mad old world went whirling on,
The Seraph breathed, and the clouds were gone ;
The clouds were gone, and she saw below
An innocent thing in a vest of snow ;
A dove that through sunshine shot with glee
To its home in the heart of a pleasant tree.
" Now speed thee, bright creature !" the Seraph said,
Ere the words were spoken the dove lay dead ;

And loud was the laugh that exultingly
Rose from the foot of the pleasant tree.

> Man's a stern Hunter !

The Seraph turned, with a holy frown,
To the wooded haunts of a mountain brown :
With a fetterless step, a stately deer
There bounded in beauty that saw no peer ;
It browzed on the red moss, it drank of the spring,
It pained not, it grieved not a living thing ;
And the pure one hoped that its days might be
From harm, as its nature from evil, free.—
The mountain echoes swelled thundering 'round
To the Forester's shout at the deer's last bound.

> Man's a stern Hunter !

O sad was her heart as that wild halloo   *
From hill-side to hill-side redoubling flew ;
Her clear glance settled, far, far away,
On a place remote from the glare of day.
There were tall trees above, and deep waters below,
With breast never heaving to ebb or to flow ;

And in that most tranquil element,
Of curious colours serenely blent,
Numberless rare shapes of life were seen,
Grateful and glad that they ever had been ;
The smile of the Seraph shed light on the lake,
As she wished it repose for its children's sake.
The song of the Fisher is heard on the land,
And death is at work on the harmless band.

                    Man's a stern Hunter !

From heaths of the hill, from depths of the glen,
Her eye sought for peace 'mong the homes of
      men ;
It fixed on a silent and lovely spot,
Where the blue wreath spun from a lonely cot,
Two children of Adam, of equal age,
There passed through the days of their pilgrimage.
They were fair as the lilies they flung at each other,
And both were the pride of a single mother.
" Be blessed !" prayed the daughter of Heaven.—A
      scream
Was heard by the little cot's garden stream ;

Of the twain on its bank there remained but one,
And he grinned like a fiend at a dark deed done.
" Oh! wo for this world of mourning and mirth !"
Sighed the Seraph, and fled from the aspect of earth`
       Man's a stern Hunter !

INSCRIPTION FOR MONUMENTS TO NEGLECTED BARDS.

HERE stands a tribute from the sculptor's hand,
To one whose birth does honour to his land ;
Would'st know whose bounty reared the work of
      pride,
Look the subscription-roll, or ask the guide ;
And would'st thou learn for whom its columns
      swell,
Read this recording tablet—it will tell.

Of a strange family, the gifted child,
Was he to whom this monument is piled ;
His tale is nothing new, he lived and died
Like all the race to which he was allied.
The world had found him heir to a hard lot,
And something more its luckier sons had not ;

Then, cheering the great impulse of his heart,
Bade him come forth and play his proper part;
Bade him come forth—as summer beams intrude
On the poor flow'ret's woodland solitude,
Luring its sweetness with a glance of fire,
To blossom for a moment, and expire.
Misled by vivid dreamings, forth he came,
And bartered life's true blessings for a name;
Spurned the contentment of a village-home,
To act a statue in a gilded dome;
Abased his majesty of mind, to gain
Exemption from nobility's disdain.
What were his triumphs?—for a day to stand
The last rare sight arrived from Wonder-land,
And soon deserted for a newer face,
To feel that, faultless, he had met disgrace,
Half deeming, with this transitory sway,
The charm that ruled his being past away.

He could not brook obscurity, so bowed
His lordly spirit to the meaner crowd;

The herd that cling to genius in decline,
As rank weeds to a long-forsaken shrine ;
Things that would rot unheeded and unknown,
If faithful to the sphere which is their own.
They fastened on him, like the sluggish beast
Which makes the generous deer a living feast ;
Urged him to haunts where good holds no control,
And turned to shame the splendour of his soul.
In pity, fate ordained this should not last,
His powers of life and pleasure failed him fast ;
And it was told, how, in a wretched shed,
Men found the Poet pennyless and dead.

Such was his course ; but now he ranks with those
Whose glory in death's desolation rose.
With him whose wit procured a royal treat
Of goodly stone, in lieu of vulgar meat ;
With him—old Scotland's son—who dropped the
            plough,
To point a stanza and to round a bow,
Plodding, before his grateful country's eyes,
Through the low labours of the vile excise ;

With him—the boy of promise—left undone
By frigid Walpole—hapless Chatterton !
These are his mates, and jointly he may claim
The equal honours of an equal fame.
Store of dull speeches and gross tavern-cheer
Shall mark his Dinner through each coming year ,
And, with his name, the sentimental sot
Will gild his homage to the frequent pot.
This is his high award, for whom arise
These glancing columns to the wondering skies ;
The spot is picturesque, and suits them well ;
Yes, and if laughter ever visits hell,
'Twould rouse a peal to shake a better sphere,
Were fiends acquainted with what's written here.

THE POET'S PRAYER.

I STAND, among the hills, alone,
  Calm, as this blessed summer even,
That my rapt heart may find a tone
  Meet to convey, its thoughts, to heaven.
In softer climes and younger ages,
  'Twas to the mountain steep and still,
Journeyed, with hermit-steps, the sages,
  Whose spirits warred with nought but ill,
And there, in holy solitude, inquired their Master's
    will.

These were indeed the wise of earth,
  Who life's consoling secret knew,
Which half dispels the gloom man's birth,
  O'er all his days of travel threw.

What must have been their lofty feeling,
   'Tranced 'midst thy cedars, Lebanon,
Or, Carmel, on thy brow revealing
   Their burning love to God alone,
When I, even I, in lowlier scenes, this hour, such
      raptures own !

Above, there's but a Northern sky ;
   Below, the humble heath in flower ;
Yet all around, Divinity !
   I trace Thy hand's transcendent power.
It is not the cold sense of duty
   Works, at this moment, in my breast,
But a deep passion for the beauty
   Through Thy mutations manifest,
Which forms its own sublime reward, and makes
      me more than blest

O little know they of the fire
   That glows within the child of song,
Who haply marking him retire
   From the dull anthems of the throng,

Think that he shares not the emotion
   Which some with saintly boldness claim ;
They little know the strong devotion
   He must inherit with his frame,—
Must with that mould of mind which gives the
     impress to his name.

Being ! whom I do feel and love,
   Seeking my nature's happiness,
Whose force no will of mine can move
   To diminution or excess,
From my soul's temple faint, but tender,
   Music is floating to the sky ;
And though nor crowd, nor solemn splendour
   Assist its feeble notes, yet I,
In humbleness, believe that Thou wilt deem it
     harmony.

My all of good Thy hand hath wrought,
   The sad, the sinful, were my own ;
Fruits of the time when Folly brought
   A willing vassal to her throne.

The good remains—the ill is parted
    Far from me, by a gulf of shame ;
And now before Thee, tranquil-hearted,
    Father of Hope ! I've learned to frame,
Out of life's lore, a creed in which fear lives not
        even in name.

THE GREAT FARCE.

AROUND me rolls a nameless mass,
 A sea of anxious men ;
I watch them as they onward pass,
 Hundreds and thousands ten.
Misguided race ! I grieve to see
That, reckless of futurity,
 You seek destruction's den ;
I grieve to think how soon this scene
Shall be as it had never been !

I look amazed upon the world :
 Here Wisdom holds its state ;
There War's red standard is unfurled,
 And Monarchs talk like Fate ;
While blistered hearts are everywhere,
And shapes of famine and despair
 On all sides congregate :

O God ! 'tis wondrous there should be
Such madness and such misery.

I mark one, in his blooming prime,
   With passion fade away ;
'Tis sad to note, at such a time,
   So fair a form decay.
I seek those eyes, whose moonlight gleam
Hath lent the melancholy beam
   Which leads his soul astray,
And find that their celestial ray
Hath power o'er nought save frenzied clay.

For what is love ?—go ask its name
   From children of the Pole ;
Or where the sun with kindred flame
   Inspires the Eastern soul :
The fires that warm the reptile's blood,
To hug its mate, and have its brood,
   Cause their blue veins to roll ;
Start not, nor turn thine head away—
   For what art thou, and what are they ?

A thousand met on yesterday
  To place a dead man's stone ;
It was triumphant holiday
  For all but me alone.
When crowds, with raptures most intense,
Brought forth their myrrh and frankincense
  To honour him that's gone,
I asked the cause of such a coil,
And laughed to scorn their pious toil.

What cares he for earth's pageantry,
  Who soundly sleeps below ?
The gifts heaped to his memory
  Might lessen living wo.
'Tis true, example draws, and then
Our light should shine before all men,
  As holy writings show :
There, there it is,—the poor display
Lures actors to the public play.

Behold yon melancholy man,
  He walks the world alone ;

Though formed on nature's choicest plan,
  Unhonoured and unknown.
O I could weep, but that his eye,
Fixed calmly, yet disdainfully,
  Seems proudly looking on,
In stern derision of the fate
Which leaves him thus to meditate.

The woes of human destiny
  May crave a human tear ;
The monster called Society
  Claims nought beyond a sneer.
The golden calf, by Folly framed,
Which man, in abject mood, proclaimed
  His god and glory here ;
The senseless idol that his power
Hath raised to rule the passing hour.

AMOR PATRIÆ.

Thou fool! I care not for the soil that bore me,
   Or more, or less, than I do care for thine;
What strand should lie beneath, what sky hang o'er
     me,
   Was Chance or Fate's allotment, and not mine;
A toad, within a rocky hollow pent,
As well might boast of its stone tenement.

I pray thee spare thy breath the dull narration
   Of holy ties to one spot linked alone;
Thou lovest thy spouse, thy offspring, and thy nation,
   For a most sovereign reason—they're thy own:
And thus the fervid sons of Afric's race
Of ebon beauty prize the lusty grace.

No land for me where things like thee are wearing
   The form that I must for a brief time wear,

The crust of every crime—I turn despairing
   From earth to dream of a dear world elsewhere,
To which the struggling spirit fain would fly,
From kindred scenes to claim nativity.

A WISH.

I HAVE a wish ungratified,
    One wish, and nothing more ;
O ! would that wish were satisfied,
    And hope and terror o'er !
'Tis not a gem from Fortune's crown
    So earnestly I crave ;
The prize I seek to make my own
    Is but an early grave.

O ! may I never live to show
    The locks of reverend grey !
But, like a vernal fall of snow,
    Ere evening, pass away ;
A sickly passenger afloat
    On a tempestuous sea ;
The motions of life's bounding boat
    Are heaviness to me.

Ay, smile, and say 'tis but the wild
    Caprice of fleeting pain ;
And that bright eyes will charm the child
    To happiness again :
Thou know'st me not ;—in vain the spark
    Of woman's love may shine ;
It cannot light a soul so dark,
    So desolate, as mine.

There is no greater misery
    For human heart to bear,
Than be condemned to live and see
    Things as they truly are ;
How Ignorance, in vulgar state,
    Proclaims the general lie,
Which Cant and Dulness consecrate,
    In base idolatry.

If there's a man who can employ
    A serious thought on earth,
May he abundantly enjoy
    The blessings of his birth.

Were he the one I loathed the most
   My blackest prayer should be,
That he, on life's accursed coast,
   Might roam eternally !

Almighty God! whose mystic form,
   By wretched mortals viewed,
Seems but the ruler of a storm,
   A reveller in blood;
I hold thee not what creeping Fear
   And Folly picture thee,
But as a friend, to dry the tear
   Of helpless misery.

Then let the elements that war
   Within me, be at peace,
And let the busy fiends of care,
   Their useless labours, cease.
From thee, the Merciful, the Great,
   An only boon I crave:
O take me from a world I hate
   Into an early grave !

THE FLIGHT OF PHILOSOPHY.

I GAZED, as is my use to do,
  One pleasant eve in June,
Upon a sky of sober hue,
  Cheered by the stars and moon.

In deep abstraction raising oft
  My looks and thoughts from earth,
With a faint hope, to find aloft
  The secret of man's birth.

That hope was nought; no new light broke
  Upon my anxious brain,
No voice through the still ether spoke
  To ease my spirit's pain.

Up rose a melancholy breeze,
  Making the blood run chill,

While, through the green tree's lattices,
  It wandered at its will.

Up rose the breeze, and I arose
  To bid the heavens adieu,
As maidens, ere they seek repose,
  In pensive mood, will do.

Ye powers, who watch o'er sinful men,
  Be merciful to me !
It is no vapour-figure then,
  Fair moon, that shadeth thee !

Nor is it aught mine eye hath seen,
  Or fancy dreamed before,
Which, light as snow, drops on the green,
  Three paces off or more.

I felt a reverential fear,
  When the dim stranger cried ;
''Tis mine to speak, and thine to hear,
  Both shall be satisfied.

Thou art, I know thou art, imbued
　With deep philosophy ;
And therefore is thy solitude,
　This hour, disturbed by me,
Who am the perfect plenitude
　Of what the Wise would be.

Upon the central world of all
　That move in mystic air,
Two had their great original,
　A transcendental pair.

They came direct from Nature's hand,
　And offspring they have none ;
For each there is a like command,
　And business to be done.

Command we have o'er worshippers
　Of knowledge grave and high ;
To us flock all philosophers
　When—as men say—they die.

Our business is to ascertain,
  Though by a different race,
That frenzy only can maintain
  Illimitable Space.

The partner of my toils pursues
  An opposite career;
'Twas his, yon nether path to choose,
  And mine, this upper sphere.

Myriads of ages have whirled past
  Since first our task had birth,
And now, delightedly, at last,
  I've reached the towering Earth.'

' The towering Earth !' I quick exclaimed,
  ' My lord, your hopes dispel,
Alas ! this sorry globe is framed
  But one point over hell,
And that is ever so inflamed
  No one its bounds may tell.'

I heard a sound, as of the wings
  Of eagles, in their flight ;
I saw a mass of shapeless things
  Thickening the vesper light,
And the dim figure rose in rings,
  Like a huge paper kite.

Just like it—for its form was thin,
  To cut the denser air,
Yet stretched out, like a parchment skin,
  To float where it was rare.

I deemed it strange he should mistake
  The bottom for the top ;
Stranger—the philosophic flake
  Of dead men's souls should drop
No word, in their long flight, to make
  Their sage conductor stop.

TO A LADY.

THOUGH my young cheek's untimely faded,
  It owes it not to cankering care ;
And though a cloud my brow hath shaded,
  Nor pain nor sorrow placed it there.

'Tis weariness of all around me,
  Which loathes, but fears to leave, the earth,
That, in its leaden grasp, hath bound me,
  To mourn no wo, yet feel no mirth.

Thy ivory hand, with music's power,
  Strikes on my heart's dull chords in vain,
Stirring the memory of some hour
  I would not have recalled again.

And vainly are thy blue eyes turning
  Their starry radiance unto mine ;

c

I've coldly greeted glances burning
   With other fires than light up thine.

Yes,—lovelier lips have bent to bless me
   Than even thy mirror sees in bloom;
Yet did they at this hour caress me,
   'Twould shed no sunshine o'er my gloom.

For, like to some unholy spirit
   Condemned to walk the world awhile,
I but the form of man inherit,
   Without his heart to sigh or smile.

O no! for I might hope to borrow
   A balsam to my soul's despair,
Could mortal joy, or mortal sorrow,
   Awake one kindred feeling there.

PAST PLEASURE.

REMEMBEREST thou the evening
  We met in the shady glen ?
'Twas the only time we ever were there,
  Or ever shall be again.
Thy eye and cheek, so beautiful,
  A glorious lustre wore ;
And deeper and quicker my young heart beat,
  Than ever it beat before.

The Sun went down unheeded
  To his chamber in the West ;
We lived in the light of each other's looks,
  And we felt that both were blest.
The far-off voice of the waterfall,
  And the bird's song warbled nigh,
Were drowned in the passionate tones that gushed
  From our bosoms swelling high.

Years have rolled by since we parted,
  Years, many a weary one ;
And I sigh for rest, as the seaman sighs
  For land, ere his course is run.
No heart is there now to love me,
  Or be beloved by me ;
Not one to stir the spirit that watched,
  In the glen's lone haunts, with thee.

I'll never forget that evening !
  No—though the thought be vain—
I would still be thine, all lost as thou art,
  Could I feel, what I felt, again.
Sorrow and shame have followed it,
  Yet, like a desolate star,
That floats in the wake of a thunder-cloud,
  Its memory shines afar.

THE BEAUTIFUL ACTRESS.

SHE plays to-night! and, therefore, pours along,
To the bright theatre, a motley throng ;
Dames of high ancestry, but rarely there,
Descend to smile upon a favourite fair :
And other dames, less lofty in degree,
Are bent to know if fair indeed she be.
Abstractedly, the youth of soft eighteen,
Sighs for the entrance of his player-queen,
Fostering the daring hope, that he may yet
Shine as the Romeo to her Juliet ;
While, by his side, the practised debauchee
Gives his loose soul to visions still more free ;
But all eyes sparkle with unusual light—
The angel-actress rules the scene to-night !

The tedious prelude's past, and she is here ;
No voice but hers attracts the public ear ;

Connubial love forgets his vows awhile,
And hangs, delighted, on her thrilling smile ;
The plighted swain, unconscious, fires the pride
Of the neglected damsel by his side,
As questioned oft, to win his truant eye,
His lip is writhed into a brief reply :
Yet blame him not, fair maid ! for he were less
Or more than man to see her loveliness,
Her step's voluptuous cadence in the dance—
Her eye's fine lightning flashing in each glance—
Those ruby portals, whence a tide of tone,
Flows, meet to issue from such source alone—
More or less far than man he were, whose gaze
Could turn, in coldness, from perfection's blaze.

But is the syren happy, who imparts
A subtile rapture to a thousand hearts ?
Oh ! yes ; look to the mimic scene ; thy sight
Is gladdened in her eye's rejoicing light.
Blest she must be whose task is to employ
Her gravest moments on a work of joy ;

But if thou yet art dubious, list the sound,
The signal of her triumph thundering 'round,
And ask of those who watch the curtain's fall,
If it descend not like a funeral pall,
Which shrouds some blighted blossom, prized in vain,
Seen for a little, and ne'er seen again!

True, true,—it is her business to be gay,
To while her own and others' griefs away;
And richly hath the admiring throng repaid
The smiler for the pleasant part she played;
But she appears in scenes more trying still,
Where nature acts without the aid of will—
All grace and archness in the Muses' dome,
How moves the Actress in her silent home?

'Tis midnight, and the workings of the mind,
In that lone chamber, need not be confined;
Nor are they; for the roses in her hair
Seem most unfitted to her brow of care;
And, strange the contrast of her tinselled state
With the lorn look which speaks her desolate,

As, from the mirror, she averts her head,
Shocked by pale lips, and cheeks of shameless red.

No longer, oh no longer ! feels she queen
Of arts that tinged with life the varied scene ;
No longer, oh, no longer ! can the smile,
Which smoothed the general brow, herself beguile
Quick from their secret cells, with added force,
Like Arab steeds impeded in their course,
Rush the reflections of a wayward life,
With all that is, and much that was, at strife :
Pain rules the hour ; remembered pleasures seem
The guilty transports of an impure dream.

It is the curse peculiar of her lot,
Still to affect the being, she is not ;
To fling a dazzling veil upon her woes,
And wear her features, as she wears her clothes.
For dark experience hath the Actress told,
A piteous tale will ne'er win public gold ;
And those who wish the crowd's applause to wake,
Must not betray it, should their bosoms ake.

'Twas once my hap by Leman's lake to roam,
And on its shore to note a rural dome,
Such as is only painted, in romance,
And rarely seen, but 'mong the hills of France:
With purple clusters, the tenacious vine
Did, lovingly, around the lattice twine;
The trellised porch, which hid the antique door,
Was jessamined and honeysuckled o'er;
In front a sheet of living crystal gave
Heaven's changeless children, mirrored in its wave;
The stalwart mountains leagued to bulwark in
One little Eden from a world of sin.
Imagination seized it for its own,
Its roof, I thought, must be Contentment's throne,
And most devoutly deemed, that, 'round its hearth,
Were ranged all virtues ever known on earth.

Alas! for the young vision! chance conveyed
My step to where my fancy oft had strayed,
And never did I disappointment bear
More unrelieved by circumstance, than there;

A sottish husband, and a slattern wife,
Waged in my paradise perpetual strife;
And cradle-music, dear domestic sound!
With kindred lays, profaned the sainted ground.

Even thus the Thespian Circe's outward guise
Of happiness, her secret mood belies.
Though laughing loves around her light lip play,
A ravening vulture eats her heart away;
Her sunny glance irradiates every breast,
But one, to her more near than all the rest:
As, throned on high, the peerless queen of night
Cheers distant worlds with showers of grateful light;
Yet, while her silver treasure copious flows,
Shares not, herself, the blessing she bestows.

ON SEEING A NETTLE SPRING FROM A LADY'S GRAVE.

I THOUGHT that on her home of death,
  Earth's loveliest plants would grow,
That Spring would twine its choicest wreath,
  Her resting-place to show.
In life all did so worship her,
I deemed the very sepulchre
  Such glorious guest would know ;
And its least dismal costume wear,
In honour of a form so fair.

But no ! she sleeps as others sleep ;
  Of flowers profusely strown,
On the fresh turf, when grief was deep,
  The odour long hath flown.
No more the envied one of all,
Who bless the bower, or grace the hall,
  She keeps her state alone ;

While o'er her nods the church-yard weed,
And foul worms on her red lip feed.

Is this, high dame ! the place of pride
    Thy flatterers promised thee ?
The slimy forms that by thee glide
    Must they thy love mates be ?
'Tis even so ; the smiling sway
Of Beauty's sceptre could not stay
    Thy step, Mortality !
In token of thy conquest, here
This rank plant riseth rude and drear.

It riseth, to all living men,
    A symbol and a sign
Of what hath been, shall be again,
    Till suns no longer shine.
Lords of the shore, and of the sea !
It treats with cruel levity,
    Your attributes divine ;
Its rampant root and loathly stem,
Whence come they ? what hath nourished them i

O wide and far extends the realm
   That rears thee from its gloom
Herb of the grave ! the Warrior's helm
   May boast its battle-plume ;
But when the triumph-tale is told,
And when the Minstrel's lip is cold,
   Regardless of their doom,
Thou'lt wave, as thou art wont to do,
   O'er Minstrel, and o'er Warrior too.

No flatterer thou,——stern honesty
   Lies in thy dark-green vest ;
Let Pride and Passion look on thee,
   And learn, and be at rest.
Should they pronounce thee vile, then tell
How she, who loved their empire well,
   But pampers thee at best ;
And ask them, while they own thy stings,
What nobler fate awaits on kings.

TO ————.

Thou wert in rosy womanhood,
　And I in life's advancing spring,
When, by thy side, a tale I read
　Of passion, sad and wildering ;

A legend of a beauteous dame,
　Bound to a cold, regardless lord,
And a poor harper boy, by whom,
　For years, that lady was adored.

We felt the tale—thou wert the bride
　Of one who cared not for thy love,
And I was young, and prized thy smile,
　All that the earth could give, above.

Where the dark chronicle had drawn
　A moving picture of the twain,

I paused, and both, in silence, traced
   The passage o'er and o'er again.

Our cheeks half met, your silken curls
   Sent tinglings to my inmost core ;
I heard the beating of your heart,
   And felt as mine would beat no more.

But when the story told, how fate
   Wrought ruin on the hapless pair,
You turned your eyes from me, and wept,
   While I pronounced a burning prayer.

Then there was bliss, new, wondrous bliss,
   As drooping on my neck you lay ;
And your soul spoke in sighs, and I
   Your tears kissed, one by one, away.

It was but for a moment's space
   Till the deep rapture dream was o'er ;
You prayed me, by our nameless ties,
   To leave you, and return no more.

And I obeyed thee, though a fire
　　Was raging in my heart and brain,
Never, from that Elysian hour,
　　To meet thy matchless glance again !

Now are my autumn days come on,
　　I stand a lonely, branchless tree ;
The revels of a kindless storm
　　Have turned me into mockery ;

But thou abidest in thy bower,
　　With goodly shoots beneath thy shade,
Whose hearts' young blossoms fill the waste,
　　By ill-returned affection made.

And 'tis the only fit of joy
　　That breaks on dull affliction's moan,
To know thou hast escaped the storm,
　　And I have felt its force alone.

Surely, whate'er my doom shall prove,
　　Whatever blight consumes my fame,

Thou wilt not smile on those who strive
  To fix derision on my name.

When thou dost bless thy youngest child,
  Thy dark-eyed boy, I hope to share,
In memory of these by-gone times,
  A portion of his mother's prayer.

MY MOTHER.

At last, O my Mother! thou sleepest!
   At last, thy poor heart is still;
No longer, dear Mother! thou keepest
   A watch in a world of ill.
Though I feel of all love forsaken,
   When thine is no longer near;
Yet I thank my God, who hath taken
   Thee hence, and I shed no tear.

I smile with a sorrowful gladness,
   While I think thou never more
Shalt drink from the black cup of sadness,
   Which, through thy whole life, ran o'er.
When a hard lot pressed severest,
   O little had been my care,
Had I known that thou, best and dearest!
   Did'st a lighter portion share.

But as there ne'er was another
　On earth more gentle and kind,
So none, my own dove-hearted mother !
　Did a heavier burthen find.
Yet it woke no voice of complaining,
　Nor changed thy passionless air,
At a time, when to image thy paining,
　Was more than I well could bear.

There needed no whisper of duty
　To summon me to thy side ;
To dwell near thy soul-stilling beauty,
　Was a rapture and a pride.
Often now, when his peace is riven,
　With visions of shame and fear,
The thought that thou'rt happy in heaven,
　Doth thy son's dark bosom cheer.

A thousand would call the spot dreary
　Where thou takest a long repose ;
But a rude couch is sweet to the weary,
　And the frame that suffering knows.

I never rejoiced more sincerely
  Than at thy funeral hour,
Assured that the one I loved dearly,
  Was beyond affliction's power.

LOVE'S PLEADING.

My fancy woos the violet,
  In stainless vest of tender blue,
And I but gaze upon thine eyes
  Because they're of its hue ;
Then, lady, shrink not thus ; for see
Thy sister-beauty smiles on me !

I kiss the honey-drops of morn
  From the fresh lip of the young rose
And I but long to try how sweet
  Is thine which like it glows :
You can't refuse this poor request,—
Your rival blushes on my breast !

THE COMFORTER.

I.

He's in hot youth, who, with a hasty step,
A heavy look, and lip which moves, but speaks not,
Strides down a mountain face, and takes his stand
Above a narrow pass.   A foe,——a foe,——
A powerful deadly foe, is pledged alone
To journey thither at the set of sun,
And he will greet him on his way.   He grasps
His blade, and pulls his beaver o'er his brow,
And turns impatient to the orb of day.
No traveller yet !—he bends him to the earth
To catch the echo of the falling foot—
All's still as death.   .
                How came that stranger there
With his long scythe, bald head, and garb of gray ?

He needs must be a bold one to confront
The armed watcher in his mood of blood !
Whate'er he be he lacks not power,—he tells
The young man to depart,—he points the path,
And is obeyed like one whose will is law.
'Tis marvellous,—the tiger-spirit yields !
The stranger takes the avenger's vow on him—
There lies the mystery.

II.

The scene is changed

To a more favoured clime.   The self-same youth,
With massier frame and cheek of darker dye,
Is leaning, pensively, where the rich moonlight
Streams on a lofty lattice.   There she sleeps,
The cherished madness of his feverish heart.
He strikes the notes of her land's minstrelsy,
And sings, in fitful strains, her peerlessness
And his o'erpowering love.   She heeds him not,—
Her heart is in the keeping of another.
He beats his forehead with extended palm,

Then speeds him, with a purpose desperate,
To a gaunt cliff that lowers upon the flood.

'Tis he again, the old man with the scythe,
The bare bald head and garb of rustic gray ;
Upon the summit of the cliff he stands,
And warns him hence, that passion-stricken son
Of a less genial soil.   He speaks of peace,
Bought by forgetfulness, which he can give,
He, who avenged the wrongs of other days,
And saved him from the fearful murder-stain,
When, in the gloomy mountain-pass, he took
The burthen of his vow.

                    He hath his will ;
The young man quits the country of his love.

III.

A mighty city and a festival—
The bells are jubilant with glad ding-dong !
And holiday-smiles are on with Sunday coats.
Thousands of joyous creatures here are met :

But who is he that mars the general mirth ?
It is the man,—it is the very man,
Though young, or strong, no longer. He is bowed
With sore infirmity,—the mountain-heath
Will never spring to his light step again !
Nor woman's beauty rack his soul with pain !
He leaves, as he best may, the giddy throng,
And, dragging his shrunk limbs to scenes apart,
Curses his fate, himself, and all mankind.

The ancient stranger, with the garb of gray,
Bald head and scythe, is by his side once more.

" I did avenge thee on thy mortal foe,
I turned thee from the last act of despair,
And now what aileth thee ?"
                          " Ills,—ills,—all ills
Which light on man in his extremity !"
" Cheer thee ! there still is hope—behold this glass ;
The sands are falling that will set thee free :
One hour thy pains are gone."

          " And who art thou,
The friend so wedded to my wretchedness ?
Whence got thy hand the strength to lay him low
Whose life was poison to me ?   Whence the balm
That eased me of affection's hopelessness ?
How hast thou skill to know my woes shall cease ¿
What is thy name ?

          Mortal ! my name is Time."

TO EVENING.

Come, Evening, come! how I long to feel
Thy balmy hand o'er my temples steal;
I shrink from the night, its fearful dream
Makes Terror's form more ghastly seem;
And I hate the summer's burning day,
Whose sun shines as if he'd shine for aye,
Luring each self-adoring worm
Forth to the scenes that its looks deform,
Mocking the face of sorrow and care,
Smiling on many a sepulchre.
Come, Evening, come! I have sought thee here,
Where the mountain-streamlet dasheth clear,
Where the solemn pine-grove riseth high,
In its native Alpine majesty;
Where of man there's nothing seen, or heard,
   Save a scarce-distinguished hum,
Soon lost in the song of thy sweet bird,—
   Come, Evening, come!

Speed, Evening, speed! on thy gentle breast
I'll lean, till my wandering soul's at rest;
Till I half forget that wrong hath been
The lord of the world I sojourn in;
And hope of the future gleams afar,
As, high in the heaven, thy favourite star.
I'll call the shades of the dear-loved dead,
And times and scenes that, for years, have fled,
I'll speak to them, while thou lingerest by,
Of all that is sacred to memory.
Perchance a silent tear or two,
Like sinless drops of thy crystal dew,
May flow from my nature's sweet excess
In a grief twin-born with happiness;
That hour my thoughts shall repose from pain,
   My bosom forget to bleed,
Then here to assume thy peaceful reign,—
   Speed, Evening, speed!

A SOUTH-SEA PARTING.

" SURELY thou dost not mean to go
   For ever from thy island maid !
And yet I've heard it must be so,
   But 'tis not truth they said :
I cannot, will not, e'er believe
   I'm doomed so deep a pang to know
Thy voice will quickly undeceive
   Those who would whisper wo."

" O that it could ! but 'tis too late
To temper, or conceal, our fate ;
Those eyes that turn to me and weep,
May note our war-bark on the deep,—
Soon, soon she'll pass into a speck,—
Would I had never paced her deck !"

" Fly from thy ocean-palace ! fly
    To shades where love hath had its fill ;
We'll seek the fan-palm's canopy,
    In clefts of the far hill.
Thy blue-eyed brothers of the wave
    Will search in vain for our retreat,
The water-spirits have no cave
    So secret, or so sweet !"

" The fearful ties thou can'st not learn,
Which bind me to my comrades stern ;
My island girl ! earth owns no spot
Their demon-power reacheth not ;
Grot, cliff, or cave, it boots not where
This foot would fly, they'd track me there.'

" Then, then, 'tis true ! no more, no more,
    For thee, shall shine Taheite's sun !
Thy step will vanish from the shore
    Where first, our souls were one.
But thou hast told me of a bower,
    In lands whose children all are fair,

If thou must hence, ah! take thy flower,
  Ah! take and plant it there."

" Blossom of life! it may not be,
My taskers call me to the sea,
And man and fate, my artless bride,
Are leagued to tear me from thy side;
I dare not stay,—words cannot tell
This moment's agony,—farewell!"

FAMILY LIKENESS.

WERE I but qualified for shining,
  In golden hues, before her eyes,
And every thing besides combining
  To make me that brutes might despise;
Yes—were I the terrestrial brother,
  To some foul shape loathed even in hell;
I do believe, sweet nymph! thy mother
  Would, for my grace, commend me well.

And were I moulded in all beauty
  Ascribed to man's least earthly form;
A soul, true to each point of duty,
  Head, cool and clear, heart, pure and warm,
But yet found wanting in the treasure,
  Thy parent's household deity,
I feel words could not mark the measure
  Of thy deep-seated scorn for me:
Now which to woo—thee or thy mother—
I know not, you're so like each other.

O THAT I WERE THE GREAT SOUL OF
A WORLD!

O THAT I were the great soul of a world!
    A glory in space!
By the glad hand of Omnipotence hurled
    Sublime on its race!
Reflecting the marvellous beauty of heaven,
    Encircled with joy,
To endure, when the orbs shall wax dim, that are given
    Old Time to destroy.

O that I were this magnificent spirit!
    Embodied to prove
The measureless bliss they were sure to inherit,
    Who lived in my love;
With elements infinite, fitted for taking
    All forms of my will;
To give me, for ever, the rapture of making
    More happiness still!

E

WELL,—I WILL NAME THEE THE LAND I LIKE BEST.

WELL,—well, I will name thee the land I like best,
The home where the foot of the pilgrim would rest;
It is not the clime where the glories of day
Give place to a night-beam, as brilliant as they;
It is not where Nature is blessed with a dower
Of all that is fairest in field, or in bower:

O no! 'tis not there that my soul hopes to be,
From the cares and the woes of its sojourn free;
But 'tis where the fancy is ceaselessly bright,
And no speck appears on its pure mellow light;
Where, better than all in the field, or the bower,
The hearts of our choice are for ever in flower.

NED BOLTON.

A JOLLY comrade in the port, a fearless mate at sea ;
When I forget thee, to my hand false may the cut-
    lass be !
And may my gallant battle-flag be stricken down in
    shame,
If, when the social can goes round, I fail to pledge
    thy name !
Up, up, my lads !—his memory !—we'll give it with
    a cheer,—
Ned Bolton, the commander of the Black Snake
    privateer !

Poor Ned ! he had a heart of steel, with neither flaw
    nor speck ;
Firm, as a rock, in strife or storm, he stood the quar-
    ter-deck ;

He was, I trow, a welcome man to many an Indian
        dame,

And Spanish planters crossed themselves at whisper
        of his name ;

But now, Jamaica girls may weep—rich Dons se-
        curely smile—

His bark will take no prize again, nor e'er touch
        Indian isle !

'S blood ! 'twas a sorry fate he met on his own mo-
        ther wave,—

The foe far off, the storm asleep, and yet to find a
        grave !

With store of the Peruvian gold, and spirit of the
        cane,

No need would he have had to cruise, in tropic climes,
        again :

But some are born to sink at sea, and some to hang
        on shore,

And Fortune cried, God speed ! at last, and wel-
        comed Ned no more.

'Twas off the coast of Mexico—the tale is bitter brief—

The Black Snake, under press of sail, stuck fast upon
 a reef;

Upon a cutting coral-reef—scarce a good league from
 land—

But hundreds, both of horse and foot, were ranged
 upon the strand :

His boats were lost before Cape Horn, and, with an
 old canoe,

Even had he numbered ten for one, what could Ned
 Bolton do ?

Six days and nights, the vessel lay upon the coral-reef,

Nor favouring gale, nor friendly flag, brought pros-
 pect of relief;

For a land-breeze, the wild one prayed, who never
 prayed before,

And when it came not at his call he bit his lip and
 swore :

The Spaniards shouted from the beach, but did not
 venture near,

Too well they knew the mettle of the daring privateer !

A calm !—a calm !—a hopeless calm !—the red sun
    burning high,
Glared blisteringly and wearily, in a transparent
    sky ;
The grog went round the gasping crew, and loudly
    rose the song,
The only pastime at an hour when rest seemed far
    too long.
So boisterously they took their rouse, upon the
    crowded deck,
They looked like men who had escaped, not feared,
    a sudden wreck.

Up sprung the breeze the seventh day—away! away!
    to sea
Drifted the bark, with riven planks, over the waters
    free ;
Their battle-flag these rovers bold then hoisted top-
    mast high,
And to the swarthy foe sent back a fierce defying
    cry

"One last broadside!" Ned Bolton cried,—deep
    boomed the cannon's roar,
And echo's hollow growl returned an answer, from
    the shore.

The thundering gun, the broken song, the mad tu-
    multuous cheer,
Ceased not, so long as ocean spared, the shattered
    privateer:
I saw her—I—she shot by me, like lightning, in the
    gale,
We strove to save, we tacked, and fast we slackened
    all our sail—
I knew the wave of Ned's right hand—farewell!—
    you strive in vain!
And he, or one of his ship's crew, ne'er entered port
    again!

PERPLEXITY.

ABOVE, below, earth, sea, and sky
Affect my spirit wondrously ;
The grass that grows, the bird that flies,
The fish that in its cavern dies,
Do, each and all, compel me still
To moods most foreign to my will,
To quests which trouble the dim brain
With prayers for light, invoked in vain !

Yet dreams, like these, might haply pass,—
I'm neither fish, nor fowl, nor grass,—
Nor care I what may be their fate,
Beyond this momentary state ;
But we, perforce, deep interest take
In self, dear self! for its own sake,—
And thoughts of man, and death, and life,
Rouse my internal world to strife.

That I have lived, that I shall die,
I do believe, but know not why,
For aught I yet have heard, or seen,
Such a strange creature should have been
With but a fraction more of evil,
I might have fairly served the devil,
And, with a dash of colder blood,
Have won the epithet of Good.

Each day some will-o'-wisp pursuing,
For ever doing and undoing ;
Perceiving, whether gay, or sad,
Man is, and ever will be, mad—
For any fit cause that appears
To call forth human smiles or tears—
Yet conscious that, in this same madness,
Exists the only chance of gladness.

Thrice blessed he, whose sluggish eye
Pries not into life's mystery,
To whom the temple is but stone,
The incense smoke, and smoke alone,

Who takes not his adventurous course
In search of Fate's forbidden source,
But, when the Sun breaks on his shell,
Admits, he serves him passing w ell !

ALTERED FEELINGS.

It gladdened me more than I well can express,
    The small river,
With its green sloping margin, which sought the caress
Of the light-hearted stroller, whose free foot to press
    It failed never.
When the warmest of months, brought the long
    happy days,
        On its bosom
The drooping laburnum still showered a blaze
        Of rich blossom :
No, I cannot express how its aspect did bless
    the heart, when first touched by its loveliness.

It gladdened me not when I saw it again,
    The small river;
It was cursed to my sense, I beheld it in pain,
Though its bright little waves, unprofaned by a stain,
    Flowed as ever ;

And the days were life-long, and the pale golden
    shower
        In profusion
Poured down as before, but away was their power
        Of illusion :
Then I marred the clear wave, and indignantly gave
    the tree and its blossoms within it a grave.

I was wrong! I was wrong! though you gladdened
    me not,
        Humble river
To cloud your fair waters, and ruin the spot
Where your drooping laburnum in golden flowers
    shot,
        Bright as ever
A maid, long adored, and this moment disdained,
        Is a token,
That in me, not in you, was the sweet spell contained
        Which is broken :
'Tis my fate to enthral my fond spirit, with all,
    on which the warm hues of its own beauty fall.

THE MOURNER.

I DO not sigh
That I catch not the glance of woman's eye;
I am weary of woman,—I know too well
How the pleasant smiles of the love-merchant sell,
To cast a serious thought on her,
Though I've been, like others, a worshipper.
I do not sigh for the silken creature,
The tinge of good, in her milky blood,
Marks not her worth, but a feeble nature.

I do not pine
That the treasures of India are not mine;
I have feasted on all that gold can buy,
I have drained the fount, men call Pleasure, dry,

And I feel the after-scorch of pain .
On a lip which would not drink again.
O ! wealth on me were nought but wasted ;
I'm far above the usurer's love,
And all other love, on earth, I've tasted.

I do not weep
That apart, from the noble, my walk I keep ;
That the name I bear, shall never be set
'Mid the gems of Fame's dazzling coronet ;
That I shall slink, with the meanest clay,
To a hasty grave, as mean as they :
The Joys of the Sepulchre do not grieve me ;
I have that, within, a name might win,
And a tomb——if such things could deceive me.

I do not groan,
Though I Life's poison-plant have known ;
Though, in my spirit's drunkenness,
I ate its fruits of bitterness,
Nor knew, until it was too late,
The ills which on such banquet wait——

'Tis not for this I cherish sadness;
I've taught my heart to endure the smart
Produced by my youth's madness.

But I do sigh,
And darkly, deeply, pine—weep—groan—and why?
Because, with unclouded eye, I see
Each turn in human destiny;
The knowledge of which will not depart,
But lingers, and rankles in my heart,—
Because it is my chance to know
That good and ill, that weal and wo,
Are words which nothing mean, below,—
Because all earth can't buy a morrow,
Nor draw from death, or the vital breath,
Aught, save uncertainty and sorrow!

A LESSON.

AWAY, while yet thy days are few, forsake thy quiet
    home,
And in a bark of buoyant hope on Life's wide
    waters roam ;
With Passion at the rudder, boy ! steer bold for
    every shore
Which to thy ardent fancy seems with sunshine
    glistening o'er,
And gladden thee and madden thee with all the
    earth can give,
Nor let thy bosom feel repose till thou hast learned
    to live.

O'er many a glancing summer wave, thou'lt find an
    island fair,
A paradise of living flowers most beautiful and rare ;

Its beacon-fires are numberless, all lighted up by
  Love,
And brighter than the brightest stars that grace
  the heavens above ;
And free to thee its flowers shall be,—the choicest
  thou may'st wear,
If thou wilt stay thy morning course, and take thy
  haven there.

If onward still thy bark must go—then onward lies
  a strand
Whose towers and domes, of burning gold, proclaim
  a royal land,—
Ambition holds a gallant sway o'er that imperial
  soil,
And, loftily, will he repay thy danger and thy
  toil :
His power can frame, from out thy name, a spell of
  joy, or pain,
To make, or mar, a nation's lot, if thou wilt bear his
  chain.

F

But if, in Beauty's fairy isle, from blossoms fondly
    pressed—

Though of all hues the sky hath known—thy soul
    should rise unblessed—

And if, in the gigantic halls that zone Ambition's
    state,

Thy heart, beneath a diamond's blaze, feel cold and
    desolate ;

And if thy will incline thee still for other shores to
    steer,

Yet no spot, like the fancied one, to welcome thee
    appear ;

Then—I implore thee, by the name thy father gave
    to thee,

And by the dust of her, who bore thy weakness on
    her knee,

That thou wilt not, however late, persuade thyself
    to stay,

In recklessness, where joy, or peace afford no lasting
    ray ;

But, though estranged, and something changed, haste
    to thy quiet home,
And spend thy days, as they were spent, ere thou
    had'st learned to roam.

BYRON.

THE cry of grief hath died·away
   Which rose upon thy fall,
And high and low have said their say
   Above the Poet's pall.
If I the latest mourner prove,
'Tis not that least, though last, in love
   I come behind them all,
But that my spirit's gift should be
The purer, and the worthier thee.

Thine was a free-born soul: it spurned
   The tyrant bonds of clay,
Felt their vile force, and inly burned
   To cast these bonds away:
And had'st thou, to thyself, been true,
And done, what thou wert pledged to do,
   I might not see to-day,

That of the herd,—thy scorn,—scarce one
But lives and laughs, while thou art, gone !

Unequal to your giant span,
   You burst the narrow shell,
In which the creeping creature, man,
   Loves punily to dwell.
Indignantly you soared abroad,
And had you left the base abode
   For ever, it were well ;
But, stooping from a sphere of pride,
Pollution touched you, and you died !

I know, 'twas on the Grecian coast—
   What business hadst thou there ?—
If hog, or dog were uppermost,
   'Twas not thy place to care.
There was no lack of knaves, or fools,
To practise Slaughter's hellish rules,
   For either of the pair ;
Heaven, in its mercy, closed thy life,
Degraded in a savage strife.

As armed, with pen of proof, to smite
   A core-corrupted age,
Recording moralists may write
   Its grossness on their page.
Though fitted least, perchance, of all
Bound by the swarming city's wall,
   A righteous war to wage ;
So he, who mocked the adoring crowd,
Before the self-same idol bowed.

The forfeit's paid,—we pardon thee,—
   Thy faults shall fade away ;
The beauty of thy memory
   Will never know decay.
Thy errors, like a cloud or two,
Upon a heaven of holiest blue,
   But intercept the ray,
To make its fervour less intense,
For trembling mortals' shrinking sense.

The Monarch of the Melody
   Is risen from his throne,

And who shall lead the harmony,
　　When he, our feast, hath flown?
His harp obeys no stranger hand,
Nor have we one whose chords command
　　The wild heart-piercing tone,
That swelled above each heavy hymn
Of those, who would have rivalled him.

Attendant on the minstrel's form,
　　A band of spirits came,
From Earth and Air, in calm, in storm,
　　In water and in flame.
The children of the Universe
Obeyed the magic of his verse,
　　And, at his will, became
Things lovely, to the wondering eyes
Which gloried in their mysteries.

He died too, as he wished to die,
　　A fair and full-grown tree,
Whose stem shot proudly to the sky,
　　And bloomed luxuriantly.

No dotage of a slow decay,
No canker of rebellious clay,
　　E'er fixed its taint on thee;
Thy spirit sprung from its abode,
In summer beauty to its God.

And in that latest, loneliest hour,
　　When human aid is vain,
There lives, for me, a thought, with power
　　To sooth the sense of pain—
The consciousness that I shall be,
In realms of immortality,
　　Permitted to obtain
A place in thy community,
With those who most resemble thee.

THE JOYS OF THE SUMMER.

O WELCOME the joys of the Summer again !
Her smile is abroad, over mountain and plain ;
The blithe birds are met in the fair forest tree,
Proclaiming, to all things, how jocund they be ;
While the faithless bee, for its amber dower,
Mocks the fond ear of the love-sick flower,
And the clustering stars, so pure and so pale,
Sympathize with the querulous nightingale,
And the flight of the young spirit knows not pain,—
The joys of the Summer are with us again !

Awake ! O awake ! 'tis the voice of the Morn ;
She comes o'er a pathway of rose-blossoms borne,
Gayly unfurling her banner of light,
Playfully chasing the phantoms of Night.
From his home in the meadows, the lark hath flown,
'Mid mountains of ether, to worship alone ;

And the wanton Sun, through the lattice peeping,
Laughs at unconscious maidens sleeping,
Who turn abashed from his frolicksome beam,
When they wake and remember the morning dream.

Away to the green-wood! away with me!
To the mossy couch, and the spreading tree,
Where, with echoless steps, through the leafy halls,
Young zephyrs are dancing at intervals,
Rouzed from repose, by the natural glee
Of the little brook piping cheerily,
Who brawls for his largess, and freely receives,
From a thousand fair flowers, a thousand leaves;
Of all that bloom by his banks, there is none
Refuses the tribute he calls upon.

Let thy heart take its rest——'tis the hour of even,
And peace is triumphant, on earth and in heaven;
The day-god reclines in his proud pavilion,
Of topaz, and sapphire, and rich vermilion:
And the breeze that ripples those locks of thine,
Is as soft, as the little palm pressed to mine;

And thy tremulous accents creep on the ear,
Like far-distant music, one pauses to hear ;
And the glory enthroned on thy cloudless brow,
Is a pledge thou art happy, as I am now !

O blessings on Summer ! she bids us rejoice ;
With her lovesome look and her lightsome voice,
She comes, in a bright robe, the hearts to cheer
Of the care-worn creatures who journey here ;
And ever she singeth a holy song,
To Life's poor pilgrims wending along :
" When storms are at work on a wild Winter day,
Droop not, despair not, ye children of clay !
For Winter will pass, with his burthen of pain,
And joy and the Summer be with you again.'

NO—COME NOT, MY LIFE.

No—come not, my life! till the gay sun is waking
  The slumbering flowers of a distant land ;
Till the pensive moon on the still heaven breaking,
  Greets, like a mother, her starry band.
As the planet of love leaves, silent and lonely,
  The coral caves of a waveless sea ;
So come to the bower, where thou art the only
  One that will ever be met by me.

Thy voice is the music of Memory, swelling,
  Through clefts, a grief-stricken heart hath known,
Like the autumn winds through some tenantless
     dwelling,
  Making, by fits, a desolate moan.

And pleasant it is, in the moments of sorrow,
   To have thy spirit to meet with mine,
That its dream may be blessed, and its dark mood
     borrow
   A beam from the holier light of thine.

Then come all alone, when the happy lie sleeping,
   When night-dews sparkle on flower and tree ;
One tear from thine eye, while our sad watch we're
     keeping,
   More than dew to the flower, will be to me.
Let the icy of soul, or the hopeful-hearted,
   Sport in the blaze of the regal sun ;
'Tis meet, love, that we, from whom joy hath de-
     parted,
   Should wait and weep when his course is run.

EPITHALAMIUM.

PRESS thy hand to this heart, love!—it feels like lead;
  I am weary of walking a journey of pain;
I'll smooth my earth-pillow, and lay down my head,
  And sleep, not to wake in this bleak world again,
Till the trump of the archangel peal through the
      gloom,
And break, with its echo, the trance of the tomb.

Nay, start not, my maiden—the mansion is poor—
  The couch not so lightsome as royal ones be;
But Death, the old warder, will stand at the door,
  And watch, through whole ages, thy lover and
      thee.
The Priest is in waiting—creep close to my side,
Nor shrink, though Eternity make thee a bride.

The night may be lonely and long—do not fear—
  We cease from all sorrow—our labour is done—
'Tis true that the loves of the worm are here,
  And spring, from our bosoms, shall many a one.
Yet, what are the masters of ocean and earth,
Save forms that are fashioned to give worms birth?

Place thy cold lip to mine, and lie close—closer still—
  Come! seal up thine eye from the false fleeting
    day—
To-night we shall slumber—ay, slumber our fill—
  From the poor wretched dreamers of life, far away—
We may laugh, when we think, that we never again
Shall see their cursed realm of sorrow and pain!

Good night to them all! Let them cloud their blue
    sky,
  And trample their green earth.—Good-night!
    Good-night!
There are few in their caves shall sleep sounder than I,
  Or care less what hour brings back the daylight,

Unheeding, though even Mortality's tread
Should mix with the reptiles to blacken our bed.

Hark !—the clock strikes the hour—adieu to thee,
  Time !
 The dotard is ringing his drowsy farewell ;
To-morrow the bells of Eternity chime,
 To sooth each wan pilgrim asleep in his cell ;
And soft, as the music of heaven, shall glide,
That chime to their spirits who lie side by side.

Thou art drooping, pale flower ! then lean on my
  breast—
 She sleeps—so the day of her trial is o'er ;
Two travellers are sped to the chamber of rest,
 To mingle their ashes, and part never more ;
Right glad of the home which refuses no guest,
Though, of sad ones, least happy, of sinners, least
  blest.

THE VIOLET.

An evil destiny, had thrown
A modest Violet, alone,
Upon a hateful spot, where rose
Each noxious weed the rank earth knows.
The giant thistle reared its head,
Contemptuous, o'er its lowly bed ;
Nettle and fatal hemlock lay
Between it and the summer ray.
In vain, it sought, with azure eye,
For skies as azure, piteously ;
In vain, with aromatic breath,
Called upon winter's grasp of death ;
Imprisoned still, it suffered long,
Unfit to cope with tyrants strong,
Its timid worth, and hapless fate,
Unseen, unvalued, till too late !

G

I found it, in an after-hour,
The wreck of a departed flower ;
But from it, not so soon to die,
The odours of its memory,
Rose o'er its tyrants' broken pride,
Now shorn and scattered, side by side ;
Nor noted, save in generous scorn,
Of the vile sway they long had borne,
Over a sad forsaken creature,
Of nobler race and kindlier nature,
Whose life had been one vain endeavour,
To gain the right, denied it ever,
The privilege to hold on earth,
A place congenial to its birth.

It was a childish thing, in wrath,
To spurn these foul weeds from my path,
To bend, with looks of earnest grief,
O'er the sear Violet's latest leaf ;
Yet in my madness there was measure,
And in my sorrow, silent pleasure.

The weeds did image to my mind,
The trampling rabble, gross, unkind,
Who bear, with envious sneer and frown,
The struggling heart of genius down.
The withered leaf, thus left alone,
Spoke of that genius, dead and gone,
While the aroma of its breath,
Proclaimed its triumph even in death.

FIDELITY IN DEATH.

IF, lady, 'tis thy fate to go
   Before me, from a world of care ;
To solitude alone, I'll show
   The love I, to thy beauty, bear.

I will not join the funeral throng,
   Nor to our wonted haunts retire,
Nor bid the Muse of grief one song,
   For memory and thee, inspire ;

But shrouded in the gloom of night,
   I'll, on the sexton, steal a march,
And, by the lantern's furtive light,
   Ensconce me 'neath the church-yard arch.

The sombre coffin-lid I'll raise,
   And stow thee, cautious, in a sack,

Then, like Æneas, from Troy's blaze,
   Speed, with love's load upon my back.

When Fame has ceased to speak thy worth,
   I'll seeth thee in a spacious pot,
With pious toil ; for though all earth
   Neglect thy ashes, I will not.

As, of the dance, thou art the queen,
   Thy neat bones shall on wires be strung,
Never, by vulgar optic, seen,
   But, in my dormitory, hung.

Thy brain I'll carefully convey
   Into a china vase, and set
The same where sunbeams liveliest play,
   Sowing it o'er with minionette.

This will display a rare conceit—
   The brain, that thinking cauliflower,
I then may, not unaptly, greet
   A tiny, intellectual, bower.

From skull of monk did Byron drain
   Deep draughts of the blood-burning wine,
But I, adored! will not profane
   With such, that gentle head of thine.

Perhaps, in pain's distressful hour,
   A sacred caudle-cup 'twill be,
Having, if aught can have, the power
   To work a miracle on me.

Lady! if thou may'st place thy trust
   In words composed of human breath,
Believe thy slave is barely just
   To his fidelity in death.

TO A CONTEMPTIBLE.

Be satisfied ; for love, or hate,
  To thee, I cannot show—
Spare further pains—I feel that fate
  Hath ruled the matter so.
To love—I must in form, or mind,
  Discover something dear ;
To hate—I must, though loathing, find
  An object worth a fear.

FIRST LOVE.

THOU think'st that nought hath had the power
　　This heart to softness move ;
Thou'rt wrong—no knight more faithfully
　　E'er wore his lady's glove,
Than I within my breast have borne
　　A first, an only love.

Her form—I cannot paint her form—
　　In life I was but young,
Even when I last knelt at her feet,
　　And on her accents hung.
I would not swear her beautiful,—
　　Yet such she must have been,—
And in my dreams of paradise
　　She mingles in each scene.

This present time, in crowded halls,
   Surrounded by the gay,
I follow, in forgetfulness,
   Her image far away ;
And if I list a touching voice,
   Or sweet face gaze upon,
'Tis but to fill my memory
   With that beloved one.

For days—for months—devotedly
   I've lingered by her side,
The only place I coveted
   Of all the world so wide ;
And in the exile of an hour,
   I consolation found,
Where her most frequent wanderings
   Had marked it holy ground.

It was not that in her I saw
   Affection's sovereign maid,
In beauty and young innocence
   Bewitchingly arrayed ;

'Twas more—far more ;—I felt, as if
  Existence went and came,
Even when the meanest hind who served
  Her father, breathed her name.

I longed to say a thousand things,
  I longed, yet dared not speak,
Half-hoped, half-feared, that she might read
  My thoughts upon my cheek.
Then, if unconsciously she smiled,
  My sight turned faint and thick,
Until, with very happiness,
  My reeling heart grew sick.

O days of youth ! O days of youth !
  To have these scenes return,
The pride of all my riper years
  How gladly would I spurn !
That form—the soul of my boy-life—
  Departed, and none came,
In after-time, with half the charm
  Which cleaves unto her name.

Nor vanished she, as one who shares
   The stain of human birth,
But, like an angel's shade, that falls
   In light, upon the earth ;
That falls in light, and blesses all
   Who in its radiance lie,
But leaves them to the deeper gloom
   Whene'er it passes by.

THE FRIEND.

I HAVE a friend,——a faithful friend,——
  His truth hath long been tried,
He moves, where'er my footsteps wend,
  A shadow by my side.
The loved of early years are gone—
  The one, of all, most dear—
Yet fly who may, he lingers on
  My last companion here.

He greets me from his hiding-place,
  In eyes that lightly roll;
I call the wine, and, lo! his face
  Is mirrored in the bowl.
It recks not where, by sea, or shore,
  On banned, or holy ground,
I rest; he pauses not before
  My presence he hath found.

But most his ever-watchful love
   Attends me in the night,
When tempests shake the spheres above,
   And stars shed forth no light :
When broods, upon a troubled brow,
   The dread of coming ill,
Then—then—I doubly feel, as now,
   That with me he is still.

Recording devil ! how he glares
   Upon me in that time,
And stamps, in burning characters,
   Each perpetrated crime ;—
And spits abasement on my cheek,
   And turns my soul from prayer.
In utter hopelessness, to seek
   A refuge in despair.

TO A DISCONSOLATE FAIR.

I CARE not though
Thy tears o'erflow
   For love of me ;
In vain thou'lt mourn,
I'll ne'er return
   To look on thee.

When last we met,
The sun had set
   On distant hills ;
The memory yet,
With wild regret,
   My bosom fills.

With smiles of love,
The stars above

Did sweetly shine,
And as they burned,
I, fondly, turned
 To worship thine.

Before that even,
I thought, that heaven
 Woke passion's flame ;
But now, too truly,
The month of July
 Tells whence it came.

The kiss you gave me,
Could not deceive me,
 My pretty one !
On cheeks of roses
Each fool reposes,
 When I am gone.

In vain thou'lt mourn,
I'll ne'er return

To look on thee ;
The tears of woman
Are far too common
A bait for me.

THE FLOWER OF MY BIRTH-DAY.

I was a wild, yet tender thing,
  In childhood's early day ;
I loved the free bird's merry wing,
The gentle tear of infant Spring,
  And the blithe look of May ;
I loved our cottage in the glen—
'Tis ruined now—'twas smiling then—

No matter !——once there was a flower
  My mother gave to me,
'Twas planted on my natal hour,
And was, of all our summer-bower,
  The favourite of the bee ;
My mother oft, in sport, would say,
" You're children of the self-same day !"

H

I prized it well—it was, in faith,
  A peerless little flower ;
I sought to shield its fairy wreath
From the chill north wind's angry breath,
  And the approaching shower ;
Blooming beneath a sunny sky,
I never dreamt to see it die.

At last, methought its roseate hue
  Waxed fainter every morrow ;
I saw it fade—the morning dew
Fell cheerly—but the flow'ret grew
  Into a thing of sorrow ;
I watched it till, by slow decay,
Its fragrant spirit passed away.

Its spirit passed—I wept the fate
  Of my poor garden-brother !
It was so beautiful a mate,
That, when it left me desolate,
  I might not find another

To rival the departed one—
My heart was in it—it was gone !

'Tis strange—Time hath sped far and fast
    Since that ill-fated flower,
Yielding its bosom to the blast,
Sickened, and drooped, and sunk at last
    Within its native bower ;
'Tis strange—how all of good, that I
Since found, hath shared its destiny.

I've marked it well—each morn hath led
    To some new cherished treasure,
Some promise-bud, which flowered and fled,
Ere the first evening sky grew red,
    With all its plighted pleasure,—
Leaving the hope-sick heart in pain,
To seek—and be deceived again.

And this is life—and this is love—
    And this is beauty's power !

And thus must fame and fortune prove,
False lights, that lead the soul to rove,
   Then vanish in an hour !
Our earliest tear and latest sigh,
Spring from one sad fatality !

A SATANIC BATTLE-CHANT.

Satan.—POWERS ! that sway the dominions of ill,
Whose bounds—thanks to man !—are increasing still,
From your thrones, in the thunder-cloud, look be-
    neath,
On the ample work of your kinsman Death ;
A host of Earth's children have met in hate,
They'll banquet, on blood, ere they separate.

Chorus of Fiends.

The better for thee !
  And the better for thine !
The wolf quits his lair,
  And the vulture speeds there,
    On their tyrant to dine.
Their fangs shall be red
In the flesh of the dead !
  Ho ! good luck to the sign !

Satan.—Powers ! whose doom is ever to bear
The wish to impart your own keen despair ;
Your pangs, while you yonder scene behold,
May loosen a moment their scorpion-fold.
See and rejoice at the blackening sky !
Hear and bid hail to the murder-cry !

Chorus of Fiends.

Hail ! Hail ! to the cry—
  Ne'er was music so sweet,
As the battle-yell,
And the bannings fell,
  When great heroes meet ;
For a name, or for ore,
To make fat, with their gore,
  The turf at their feet.

Satan.—Powers ! whose sole joy's to people well,
With slaves, the bitumen soil of hell,
Pray that Earth's reptiles may never know,
How madly they work each other's wo,

Damning themselves for a specious name,
Religion—Liberty—Fortune—Fame!

Chorus of Fiends.

May the wretched race,
  To the last, never see,
'Tis a lie that leads
To whatever deeds
  Engender misery ;
And ne'er may they know
How little of wo,
  Did love rule them, would be

STRANGE NUPTIALS.

BELOW the cheerful surface of the earth,
Within a dank and dismal charnel-vault,
I sat a lonely watcher.   It was still,
Beyond what dead men's homes are used to be.
Forgetful of the upper air, and eve
Of summer, dozed in heaviness the bat ;
The toad lay torpid in its slimy lair,
The briny drippings of the arch had ceased,
And even the ravening worm, gorged at length,
Paused, for a little, from its loathsome feast,
And coiled itself within a putrid bower.

Coffins lay 'round me with their mouldering heaps
There were such multitudes, I could not guess
How many there might be ; for, though a light
Of subtile vivid green, unnatural,

Proceeding whence the dead alone could tell,

Made nearer things to vision palpable,

Yet, in the far-off distance of the vault,

That strained the sight to measure, this strange
     light,

Faded in darkness, which, with it compared,

Seemed holy.

       But of all I gazed on there,

Two forms divorced from life, and in a niche

Placed near each other, though most opposite

In what, on earth, do wide distinction make,

Sex, and the term of years, and outward pomp,

Fixed my especial wonder.   They did lie

Raised high above their gloomy tomb-fellows ;

Lids there were none on their sarcophagi,

Which showed like variance in the workmanship

As, in their aspects, those who slept within.

The one contained a corpse of hideous feature,

On which disease, and time, and cruel passions

Had wrought their worst. 'Twas once an aged man,

And life's vain splendour cleaved unto him still ;

Stones, the most precious, mocked the rigid brow,
Rich swathings, from the cunning Indian's loom,
Encompassed him ; and of the burnished gold
His grave-bed, broad and massy, had been framed.
The other, a thin shell of common wood,
Girt, in white weeds, what erst had been a maid—
A village-girl, nipped in her April beauty,
By freezing, pitiless Death.   'Twas my fate
To watch, perforce, beside this fearful pair.
Sudden the elfin light of ghastly green
Forsook the distant windings of the vault,
And settled, with a hateful brilliancy,
In the same niche where the two corpses lay.
Then rose the strangest music ever heard
By ear of living man.   It was so low,
I could not say I felt the silence broken,
And yet it pierced the inmost core of sense,
Thrilling with joy, most like a pleasant madness.
The author of that wondrous minstrelsy
Showed, I doubt not, his potence in the scene
Which followed at its close.

As I expect

To meet my Maker at a judgment-seat,
With the last note of awful melody,
I saw the rich-clad corpse of the old man
Sit upright in the coffin ; yet no more
Of life, in its grim visage, than had been
Heretofore, save that now two glairy eyes,
Mashed by foul putrefaction, were unveiled,
And they did rest upon the clay-cold girl,
Who, as if stirred by an all-powerful spell,
Rose likewise in her shroud, and bared the things,
Which once received God's blessed light, and gave
Gladness to all they looked on.   Then there came
Voices from out the blue lips of the twain,
Speaking that I dare not repeat, what fiends,
Alone, could utter in their damned mirth ;
But what the theme was I may tell—'twas love !
Ay, love from gelid corpses !

The old man,

Rich clad, did seem to call on the young maid,
Cinctured in humble cerements, to partake

His gorgeous coffin, as a bridal bed.

Long communed they, with monstrous form of speech,

As lovers, in perdition's pit, might commune,

Till she, the maid, consented to be his.

Then flamed, to paining, the thin light of green.

I closed my eyes, just while a star might twinkle;

The old corpse and the young lay side by side,

In the broad grave-bed of red burnished gold,

When they were oped again.

        The thin green light waxed dim;

But, by its fading gleam, I saw the pair,

Embedded in their rottenness, embrace,

And heard the meeting of their clammy lips,

And a hell-peal rung to their wedding joys;

And I did shriek, even as a dying man,

Whose last word is despair! and then awoke,

And blessed myself, wiping my cold damp brow.

It was high noon. Loud chimed the village-bells,

With merry music, on my waking ear,

And to the question, "Why these sounds of mirth?"

There came a quick reply: " Master, Od's pity !
You o'erslept yourself!—sure the cross old Squire,
Who coins an oath for each day i' the year,
This morn, in spite of his fast friend, the gout,
And summers seventy notched upon his front,
Led to the church the parson's youngest daughter,
The pretty mistress Jane.   Her father's poor,
And if she love another, as some say,
Why she can marry him, when old one's gone."

My dream—my dream—my horrid dream—was
    read !

A PEEP AT FORTUNE.

SCENE, *A wretched Hut on a Heath*—TIME, *Mid-night.*

NICHOLAS, *a reputed Wizard,* solus.

Enter YOUNG VAUNTINGTON *in Disguise.*

Nich. WHAT would'st thou in the hut of an old man,
That rudely thus, at night's most solemn hour,
Thou dost intrude thy presence?

Y. Vaun. Good master,
Pray excuse me, if, without book-learning,
I do make mistakes—honest, though rough, am I;
As for my business, that I'm sure thou knowest
Better than I can tell.

Nich. Again, I ask,
What would'st thou in the hut of an old man?

Y. Vaun. Well, since I must, I must.—In good
       sooth, Sir,
But under favour of thy famous craft,—
Which I do much respect,—if, as 'tis said,
Thou art acquainted with futurity,
Or him who knows it, be he black, or white,
I care not, I shall live thy grateful slave,
If thou wilt give me, a poor village lad,
A peep at coming fortune.

   Nich. Modest youth,
By the complexion of thy natal star,
Great things, and soon, I find, are waiting thee.
At the first breaking of the morning dawn,
Thou shalt arouse thee to the hunter's horn,—
A jocund train shall own thee for their lord,—
A mettled courser bear thee far a-field,
And men will call thee young Squire Vauntington,
Sir Philip's son, whose pleasure it hath been
To masquerade in groom's habiliments,
And break his jest on age and penury.

Y. Vaun. Sharp-sighted seer ! they make false
    reckoning
Who count on cheating thee.   But to the point.
Though I have wrapt me in a menial's weeds,
I come no menial's errand.   Nicholas,
The world avouches, and I do believe,
That thou hast learned,—how it imports me not,—
To penetrate the dark and teeming depths
Of unsunned time, and with a lucid glance
To note the image of what is to be.
There is a thing on which my heart is set,—
Nor set in sport, but sober thoughtfulness,—
Thy art can help me to it.

Nich. Name it, Sir.

Y. Vaun. I need not tell thee how, by birth alone,
A world of hope is mine.   This is well known.
But my soul plumes her for a nobler flight
Than the unlaurelled state of ancestry.
Most think me eloquent—I know I'm young—

Brave enough too, and something popular—
Generous perhaps, nor hated by the sex,
Whose favour's better than a barony ;
And sure, a concert of such notes as these
May well keep Fortune dancing at my heels.
But more—I have within that confidence,
That high assurance of complete success,
Which earth's exalted never were without,
And which, in truth, is three-thirds of life's battle.

Nich. Whither leadeth this ?

Y. Vaun. To the conviction,
That infant fancies will grow into facts ;
That I shall stand in fate's good hour erect,
Where even the haughtiest of our antique name
Had gladly bent the knee.

Nich. Well, be it so—
Success attend thee and thy aspirations !

Y. Vaun. Thy manner smacks of mockery, old man.

I

Nich. Not mockery, good youth, but weariness :
I pr'ythee make me master of thy wish,
Or cease to break upon my quietude.

   Y. Vaun. My wish runs briefly thus.   Reveal
      to me,
Through the potential spirit of thine art,
A portraiture of what the time will show
When my young honours reach maturity,
And nothing can be added to their growth :
Give me to see myself with a true sight,
As, at that moment, I shall seem to all
Who gaze upon my greatness.

   Nich. Could I grant
What thou dost ask, in sooth 'twould serve thee
      nought.
But, even say increase of happiness
Would follow the fulfilment of desire,
How should a frail obscure memorial
Of Time's career, and Fortune's perverseness,
Compass so strange a matter ?

Y. Vaun. Hark ye, Sir !
I have not sought, nor will accept, thy counsel,
Regarding what may be, or well, or ill,
For my high state to know.   I am assured
The power is thine to do the thing I ask.
If, like a gracious wizard, you comply,
Five pieces of the red gold shall be thine ;
But if thy seer-ship choose dull obstinacy,
By good St George I swear, at a cart's tail,
Unless thy black liege hasten to the rescue,
I'll have thee soundly whipt.

Nich. Ho ! ho !—ho ! ho !
What, have me scourged, Sir, scourged, and placed
        i' the stocks,
For pastime to the rabble !—you but jest,
Just as I did when I framed my answer—
Enough of these loose words—I'll to the work !
Let's see ; thou would'st, I think, behold thyself,
As thou shalt to the admiring world appear
At the blest moment when tired Fortune saith
My task is perfected—I can no more !

Y. Vaun. Most true—I would—I would.

Nich. Come, stand then here ;
Move not thy foot from off this sable mantle.
'Tis well—now fix thine eye right on the moon.

(*He gazes on the moon while* NICHOLAS *mutters an
incantation ; at the conclusion of which, he places a
pitcher of water before* YOUNG VAUNTINGTON.)

Nich. It prospers—thou'rt a favourite of the stars—
Enough—enough of moonlight !—bend thy knee,
Still resting on the mantle.—What do'st mark ?

Y. Vaun. (*Looking into the pitcher.*)
A mirror, larger and more beautiful,
Than e'er was fashioned by Venetian skill.

Nich. Owns not that mirror some strange qualities ?

Y. Vaun. It does ! it does !—clearer it seems than
        crystal,

Yet, to my eye, reflection gives it none!——
Now a soft haze is gathering on its surface——

Nich. Keep thy glance steady, else we toil in vain.
Watch well the haze,——'twill disappear anon.

Y. Vaun. 'Tis gone already—God! how like to life
Is this brave fiction of thy matchless skill!

Nich. Thine eye doth sparkle in the quiet light
Of the night's noon—what vision gladdens thee?

Y. Vaun. Another Eden! an unrivalled scene!
Whose perfect parts compose a heavenly whole—
This truly is deception's masterpiece!
The purple hills lie dimly in the distance;
Yet, by some sweet device, my sight takes in
All, even the sheep which pasture on their slopes.
Oaks, sturdy chieftains of the olden time,
List the stern music of the cataract,
And rear their crests, as if prepared to face
The heavy onslaught of the winter-storm.

The soil is quickened with fertility,
And vegetation showers most bountiful
Its richest juices in the fairest shapes,
Within this lovely landscape's princely bounds.
The deer, that riot in the ample chase,
Seem not unconscious of their owner's lot,
So taperingly they bear their untamed heads.
Lakes, rivers, and star-gleaming waterfalls,
Green woods, and flowering meads, and sudden glades,
Apparelled are in hues of mutual beauty.
To talk of gardens, where all looks like one,
Were vain perhaps ; yet there's a spot so bright,
So exquisite, where every thing is rare,
That I'll describe it by comparison,—
A priceless diamond set in purest gold !

Nich. The grounds will do.   What say'st thou
   to the mansion ?

Y. Vaun. The mansion !—there is none !

Nich. Nay, Sir, there is,

And one whose regal style of architecture
Doth mingle deftly with the sylvan pomp
Of the surpassing landscape, which awakes,
What I must call, the wonders of thine eloquence.

Y. Vaun. Quick ! let me see it then. In faith 'tis
  here !
By my best hopes, a proper dwelling-place !
This is the fitting harmony of taste :
The stately columns' Greek magnificence
Is rightly wedded to the fairy site.
In such a dome as this, one could not feel
The vulgar ills that wait on vulgar life.

Nich. Thou'lt know betimes. Fate says, the
  lordly pile,
The broad domain, from the remotest hill
To the first field, with the umbrageous woods,
Exuberant meads, transparent streams and lakes,
Gardens, the cabinets of many a gem,
Prized by more sense than one, shall yet be thine—
This Fate says, and I swear !

Y. Vaun. I dreamt as much,
And, for externals, rest me satisfied.
But, Nicholas, where am I ?—haste ! show me.
My chief wish was, to view my proper self,
As men shall view me when the pinnacle,
The golden point of life's advancement's, gained.

Nich. Read me the mirror. Tells it no new tale ?

Y. Vaun. A new one and a strange one ! There's
        a whirl,
As all were far from right, within the mansion,
Where the scene lieth now.   Above, below,
With the rapidity of thought, are shown
Suites of imperial rooms, wanting in nought,
Claimed by the state domestic, but the light
Of human faces in the mood of joy.
Why, there's no lord to do the honours here !
But wretched menials, few and hunger-stricken,
With tapers in their hands, creep through the halls,
Which seem, at once, vast, grand, and comfortless.

Nich. I pray you to peruse the mirror well.

Y. Vaun. Ne'er trust me but I do. Another
   change!
An aged man at prayer, kneels in his night-dress;
A single lamp scarce shows the dusk apartment,
Of spacious size, and with odd furnishing
On its high walls, of gaping blunderbuss,
Small sword and broad, and pistols hung in pairs,
Ill gear, methinks, for a saint's neighbourhood!—
In faith I wrong him! for he prayeth not,
But bends him o'er his hoarded money-bags,
His arid fingers poising each dear coin,
As though it had the health-sustaining virtue
Given by crazed chemists to their fabled stone.
Beyond all doubt, this is the griping steward;
Look how he chuckles o'er the spoils of place!
Well done, old sinner! what a rogue it is!
He must to bed, and to secure his love,
He tugs it forth from its diurnal prison,
Stowing it 'neath the pillow. How he shakes

All over with the miser's passion-fit,
Whose marks lie deeply in his verjuice visage,
Commingled with infirmity and fear.
Now he makes fast each doubtful bolt, and trims
His feeble lamp, and draws his weapons nigh.

As one to serve me in an after hour,
I like not this skin-dried anatomy,
Whose blasted form seems to have left the grave
To keep its watch in penance for the past.

Nich. He thinks himself as distant from the grave
As thou ; and, what is more, thy equal, Sir.

Y. Vaun. Would that I saw the face with youth
          upon it !
I tell thee, whatsoever he might think,
His damned avarice should not feed on me.

Nich. Then note his aspect ere the moon goes down.
          (*The Moon is seen sinking behind a hill.*)

Y. Vaun. The face! accursed juggler! 'tis my
    own!

    (YOUNG VAUNTINGTON *rushes out, overturning
    the pitcher.*)

Nich. Hallo! why frightened at your age's grace?
You've cracked my only pitcher, and retained
The five broad pieces which you promised me.
I've given you all you asked, a pleasant peep
At your proud fortune's rich maturity.
Haply thou'lt wedge old Nicholas in the stocks!
Or at the cart's tail whip him!—Ho! ho! ho!

SONGS.

SONGS.

THOU KNOW'ST IT NOT, LOVE.

THOU know'st it not, love, when light looks are
    around thee,
  When Music awakens its liveliest tone,
When Pleasure, in chains of enchantment, hath
    bound thee,
  Thou knowest not how truly this heart is thine
    own.
It is not while all are about thee in gladness,
  While shining in light from thy young spirit's
    shrine,

But in moments devoted to silence and sadness,
   That thou'lt e'er know the value of feelings like
      mine.

Should grief touch thy cheek, or misfortune o'ertake
      thee,
   How soon would thy mates of the Summer away !
They first, of the whole fickle flock, to forsake thee,
   Who flattered thee most when thy bosom was gay.
What though I seem cold while their incense is
      burning,
   In depths of my soul I have cherished a flame,
To cheer the loved one, should the night-time of
      mourning
   E'er send its far shadows to darken her name.

Then leave the vain crowd,—though my cottage is
      lonely,
   Gay halls, without hearts, are far lonelier still ;
And say thou'lt be mine, Mary, always and only,
   And I'll be thy shelter, whate'er be thine ill.

As the fond mother clings to her fair little blossom,
The closer, when blight hath appeared on its bloom,
So thou, love, the dearer shalt be to this bosom,
The deeper thy sorrow, the darker thy doom.

K

THE PIRATE'S SERENADE.

My boat's by the tower, my bark's in the bay,
And both must be gone ere the dawn of the day ;
The moon's in her shroud, but to guide thee afar,
On the deck of the daring's a love-lighted star ;
Then wake, lady ! wake ! I am waiting for thee,
And this night, or never, my bride thou shalt be !

Forgive my rough mood ; unaccustomed to sue,
I woo not, perchance, as your land-lovers woo ;
My voice has been tuned to the notes of the gun,
That startle the deep, when the combat's begun ;
And heavy and hard is the grasp of a hand
Whose glove has been, ever, the guard of a brand.

Yet think not of these, but, this moment, be mine,
And the plume of the proudest shall cower to thine ;
A hundred shall serve thee, the best of the brave,
And the chief of a thousand will kneel as thy
slave ;
Thou shalt rule as a queen, and thy empire shall last
Till the red flag, by inches, is torn from the mast.

O islands there are, on the face of the deep,
Where the leaves never fade, where the skies never
weep ;
And there, if thou wilt, shall our love-bower be,
When we quit, for the greenwood, our home on the
sea ;
And there shalt thou sing of the deeds that were
done,
When we braved the last blast, and the last battle
won.

Then haste, lady ! haste ! for the fair breezes blow,
And my ocean-bird poises her pinions of snow ;

Now fast to the lattice these silken ropes twine,
They are meet for such feet and such fingers as thine.
The signal, my mates—ho ! hurrah ! for the sea ;
This night, and for ever, my bride thou shalt be !

I'LL TELL THEE THE HOUR.

I'LL tell thee the hour I love the best—
When the Sun sleeps upon Ocean's breast,
When evening echoes repeat the tale
That's told by the wakeful nightingale,
When through the forest the green leaves lie
At rest on their branches droopingly,
   And, in worlds above,
No star is abroad, but the star of Love.

I'll tell thee the spot where I would be
When this holy hour descends on me,
By the deep glade in a lone retreat,
Where the sweetest flowers are sure to meet,
Where the jasmine, circled round and round,
Is still with the amorous woodbine found,
   And no one is near
To dash from the wild rose the starting tear.

I'll tell thee the one I'd have to share,
At that blest time, in a scene so fair,
The downcast glance of whose bashful eye
Would lend to twilight a softer dye,
Whose tone, half-heard, in its passionate tale,
Would charm to silence the nightingale ;
              'Tis thee, Mary ! thee !
I'd have at that hour alone with me!

I WOULD NOT HAVE THEE DRY THE TEAR.

I WOULD not have thee dry the tear
 Which dims thine eye of blue,
I would not that thy cheek should wear
 A smile at our adieu.
Yet cheer thee, love !—the past was bliss,
 And though we part in pain,
A happier hour will follow this,
 And we shall meet again.

O think not that the wild sea-wave
 Shall bear my heart from thee,
Unless its cold breast prove my grave,
 'Twill work no change on me.
The troubled music of the deep
 Is now our farewell-strain,
And fond affection well may weep,
 Yet I'll return again.

I go to seek a bower of peace
   In lovelier lands than thine,
Where cruel Fortune's frowns shall cease—
   Where I may call thee mine ;
And when, to crown my fairy plan,
   But one thing shall remain,
Then, love, if there be truth in man,
   I will return again !

PAGE'S SONG.

THE Baron is lord of a royal domain,
With many good lances his right to maintain,
And gallant alike at the battle, or board,
He drains the last flagon, he draws the first sword ;
But, far above all, he's the sire of a maid,
Whose glance dims the flash of the Baron's best blade.

I serve not the Baron—I wait at the call
Of his beautiful daughter in bower and hall ;
Aroused to the chase, by her palfrey I stand,
With hound at my foot, and with hawk on my hand,
And in festival-hours, the duty is mine,
To strike the glad harp, and present the red wine.

When near her, a thousand thoughts whirl through
        my brain
Sometimes full of pleasure, sometimes full of pain ;

I mark, on the goblet, the print of her lip,
And kiss it away as in secret I sip ;
Yet I tremble to touch but her glove, and I sigh,
Like a sad stricken deer, when her wooers are nigh.

Ah ! loud were the jest, from the knight to the squire,
Did they hear how a poor silly page dare aspire ;
But bound shall my soul, like a shaft from the bow,
Ere one, on the broad earth, that secret shall know,
Though hard I'll still think it, that beauty should prove
The prize of high fortune, and not of true love.

O FOLLOW HER NOT!

O FOLLOW her not! O follow her not!
   Though she lure thee with smile and song;
Fair is her cheek, but her heart is black,
   And the poison of death's on her tongue;
She'll leave on thy innocence many a blot—
Then follow her not! O follow her not!

Some call her Pleasure, and some call her Sin,
   Some call her a Lady gay,
For her step is light, and her eye is bright,
   And she carols a blithesome lay.
" Away to the bower where care is forgot!"
But follow her not! O follow her not!

Though her step invite, though her eye burn bright,
   Though green be the leaves in her bower

Yet that step is false as a meteor-light,
   And that eye hath the rattle-snake's power.
Her bower! O wild and unblessed is the spot—
Then follow her not! O follow her not!

WHY STOOD I FIXED?

WHY stood I fixed, as the slave of a spell,
Listening the notes that were warbled so well?
'Twas that to fancy they summoned a scene,
Lovely and happy, and thou wert its queen!

Why, in the valley, when Morn was awake,
Watched I the small ripple dimple the lake?
Why longed a home by its waters to share?
'Twas from the deep wish to dwell with thee there!

And why, at this hour of silence and night,
Glows my full heart in the snowy moonlight?
'Tis from the hope of our meeting on high,
Even should the light of these day-visions die.

I HEAR IT YET.

I HEAR it yet, that bugle-note,
Far down our peaceful valley float ;
And 'tis the self-same mournful blast
    They blew, the very day
My love upon me looked his last,
    And went away.

Again it peals—so wild a strain
Were fitter for the battle-plain :
Alas ! 'tis thence, indeed, it comes,
    Mixed with the cannon's roar,
And maddening shouts, and deafening drums,
    Heard evermore !

No marvel they should haunt me still,
In sadness, wander where I will,

These notes, to love's last deep adieu,
  So closely, darkly bound ;
No marvel if all senses grew
  Absorbed in sound.

O wo ! his was a bloody bed !
With Spain's far earth beneath his head ;
Not one to watch by him, and mourn,
  Not one to say, farewell !
But that heart-breaking bugle-horn,
  And battle's swell !

THOUGH MINE ARE THE YEARS.

THOUGH mine are the years of the young and the gay,
Yet I have not the heart to proceed on my way;
O where is the beacon inviting me on !
This moment I neared it—and now it is gone !
> Much may I suffer,
> Far may I roam,
> But the Traveller never
> Can find a home !

Down by the green bank, the violets spring,
Far in the forest, the merry birds sing ;
The wild rose is blushing in proud purity,
Turning her cheek from the kiss of the bee ;
> Each has its kindred,
> All have their home,
> But the Traveller ever
> Is doomed to roam !

I've journeyed, since morn, in quest of a spot
Where the pure-hearted dwell, and the vile are not ;
The walks of the world I have wandered o'er,
But my search is vain, and I'll toil no more :

      Scorched in the desert,
      Dashed on the foam,
      The Traveller never
      Can find a home !

I've heard there is rest for the wearied one,
Where the rank grass grows by the church-yard
      stone ;
When the shadows of Even are all abroad,
I'll lay me down there in my last abode ;

      Glad that, no longer
      Condemned to roam,
      The Traveller at last
      Shall find a home.

I CRAVE NOT A PROMISE.

I CRAVE not a promise, I ask not a token,
In pledge of a faith to be always unbroken;
I know thy affection will never depart,
While the flame of true love burns clear in thy heart;
And should it grow dim, may mischance overtake me,
If, more than the light breeze, thy falsehood will shake
       me !

Nor think that I dream of a license for ranging,
Though sealing no vow, and no love-gift exchanging;
My passion, for thee, sprung not up in a night,
To die in the blaze of a single day's light;
It rose with a sense of thy worth, and shall blossom
While that keeps its place, as at first, in thy bosom.

Then leave, to Love's children, the vow and the token,
We may yet think it meet that our ties should be
      broken;

Neither symbol, nor oath, could my free spirit bind,
If it found that deception had tainted thy mind;
Nor would I, maid, have thee to cling to me longer,
Should'st thou meet one whose passion was truer, or
     stronger.

NAY, SWEET, IF THOU LOVEST ME, MIX NOT IN THE DANCE.

NAY, sweet, if thou lovest me, mix not in the dance !
Though to grace it to-night
Flock the high and the fair ;
Yet go not ! O go not !
In its madness to share,
To change thy calm look for a Circean glance !—
Nay, sweet, if thou lovest me mix not in the dance !

I worship the light of thy spirit alone,
And ne'er would I see thee,
So deprived of its rays,
As thou must be, when lost,
In that blood-stirring maze ;
There never was woman more lovely, I own ;
But, O, 'tis thy spirit I worship alone !

Believe me, 'tis not for thy faith that I fear ;

    I care not, though round thee

      Fashion's gayest bands move,

    And smilers, by hundreds,

      Take the palm of my love:

If true to thyself, thou'lt thy nature revere,—

O trust me, 'tis not for thy faith that I fear !

Then, sweet, if thou lovest me, mix not in the dance !

    Alone, in thy beauty,

      Give thy voice to the song,

    Or go forth and dazzle

      Where fairest ones throng ;

But change not thy step, the still might of thy glance,

For the frenzy that whirls, and leers in the dance

WHY WALK I BY THE LONELY STRAND?

Why walk I by the lonely strand?
   He comes not with the tide,
His home is in another land,
   The stranger is his bride.
The stranger, on whose lofty brow
   The circling diamonds shine,
Is now his bride, whose earliest vow,
   And pledge of hope, were mine.

They tell me that my cheek is pale,
   That youth's light smile is gone ;
That mating with the ocean gale
   Hath chilled my heart to stone ;
And friendship asks what secret care
   There is to work me wo,
But vainly seeks a grief to share
   Which none shall ever know.

Ye waves, that heard the false one swear,
　　But saw him not return,
Ye'll not betray me, if a tear
　　Should start in spite of scorn.
Yet, no—a wounded spirit's pride,
　　Though passion's pangs are deep,
Shall dash the trait'rous drop aside,
　　From eyes that must not weep.

In vain, alas! I have no power
　　To quit this lonely strand,
From whence, at the wild parting hour,
　　I saw him leave the land.
Though he has ta'en a stranger bride,
　　My love will not depart ;
Its seal, too strong for woman's pride,
　　Shall be a broken heart !

WOULD'ST KEEP THE DEEP DYE OF THINE EYE IN ITS BRIGHTNESS?

WOULD'ST keep the deep dye of thine eye in its
    brightness?
Thy cheek in its love-hue, thy step in its lightness?
Thy heart that lies sleeping, with hope for its pillow,
From shock of the blast, and from bound of the
    billow?
           Then come not with me!
My spirit is wilder than storm of the sea!

Would'st have a fair home,—see each sun set in
    gladness,
And morning awake thee,—but never to sadness;
Where thy life, all unrippled, might wimple away,
Like a pure little stream on a soft summer day?
           Then flee, maiden! flee!
Go wed with the whirlwind, but mate not with me!

But wouldst thou, to gain thee a bliss without telling,

Take far in the desert thy desolàte dwelling,

And worship the fierce-flaming orb which rose o'er
thee,

Though frenzy should follow the smile that he bore
thee?

Away then with me !

No spouse, for the rover, more fitting can be !

IT WAS NOT FOR THE DIAMOND RING.

It was not for the diamond ring upon your lily
    hand,—
It was not for your noble name,—it was not for your
    land,—
I saw no gem, no lordly name, no broad domain
    with thee,
The day you stole my trusting heart and peace of
    mind from me.

You came—I knew not whence you came—we met—
    'twas in the dance—
There was honey in each word of yours, and
    glamour in each glance;
Though many were around me then, I nothing saw
    but him,
Before whose brow of starry sheen fresh-fallen snow
    were dim.

You're gone !—it was a weary night we parted at
    the burn ;
You swore by all the stars above, that you would
    soon return ;
That you would soon return, light love ! and I your
    bride should be,
But backward will the burnie roll, ere you come
    back to me !

They say, that soon a smiling dame of lineage like
    to thine,
Will take thee by the fickle hand, thy falsehood
    placed in mine ;
The music and the rose-red wine to greet her will
    appear—
For wedding-song, a sigh I'll have—for bridal-
    pledge, a tear.

O would that thou had'st passed me by, in coldness
    or in pride !
Nor wrought this deadly wrong to her, who on thy
    truth relied :

The hunter's to the greenwood gone, his spear is in
     its rest,

But he'll not wound the trusting dove, that shelters
     in his breast.

NATIONAL SONGS.

NATIONAL SONGS.

THE IRON DESPOT OF THE NORTH.

THE iron Despot of the North
    May on his vassals call,
But not for him will I go forth
    From my old castle hall.
Though sabres, swayed by Polish hands,
    Have battled for the foe,
There's one, at least, Oppression's bands
    Shall ne'er see brandished so !

I fought in Freedom's farewell field,
    I saved a useless life ;
No weapon from that hour to wield,
    In a less noble strife.

When hostile strangers passed my gate,
   On Hope's red grave I swore,
That, like my ruined country's fate,
   This arm should rise no more.

I flung into the bloody moat,
   A flag no longer free,
Which centuries had seen afloat,
   In feudal majesty.
The sword a warrior-race bequeathed
   With honour to their son,
Hangs on the mouldering wall unsheathed,
   And rust consumes my gun.

The steed that, rushing to the ranks,
   Defied the stubborn rein,
Felt not on his impatient flanks,
   The horseman's spur again.
And I, the last of all my line,
   Left an affianced bride,
Lest slaves should spring from blood of mine,
   To serve the Despot's pride.

TELL ME NOT OF STAMBOUL'S TOWERS.

TELL me not of Stamboul's towers,
    Rising o'er the sea ;
Fields there be whose simplest flowers
    Are more dear to me.
Home of bliss, once wildly straying,
Where thy pleasant brooks are playing,
    Oft I turn to thee ;
Fate may sever us for ever,
    But the spirit's free !

Still, when Eve its curtain closes,
    By the star-light pale,
In my own loved Georgia's roses
    Sings the nightingale.
'Mid these scenes of hateful splendour,
Fancy hears that music tender

M

In my native vale ;
Tears awaking while 'tis speaking
  Its most mournful tale.

Though the Turkish lord hath bound me
  With a golden chain,
Other, dearer ties are round me,
  And I pine in pain.
In the palace there is sadness,
And, its queen, the voice of gladness
  Welcomes not again:
Grandeur grieves me—Hope now leaves me—
  Love and Life are vain !

O FOR THE MERRY MOONLIGHT HOUR!

O FOR the merry moonlight hour !
   O for the hearts that warmest glow !
O for the breath of the summer flower,
   Far floating in the vale below !
Hail to the clime where Beauty's power
   Is stamped on every plant and tree ;
Joy's rosy throne—Love's wedding bower—
   Land of our choice, fair Italy !

O for the dance !—the dance at even !—
   Woman's smile is loveliest then ;—
O for the notes which came from Heaven,
   Which came—but ne'er returned again.
Blessed be these notes ! they long have striven
   To keep the young heart warm and free ;
And never was boon to mortals given,
   Like the song of fervid Italy.

O for the morn ! the glorious morn !
   When souls were proud, and hopes were high,
Ere the Eagle's fiery plume was torn,
   Or his course grew dark in the western sky.
That wild bird's wing is shrunk and shorn,
   Yet our empire winds from sea to sea ;
Fame's wandering torch o'er earth is borne,
   Love's, shines alone for Italy !

Then hail to the merry moonlight hour !
   And joy to the hearts that warmest glow !
Ever bright be the bloom of the summer flower,
   And sweet its breath in the vale below !
And long may our maidens' evening bower
   Echo the song of the gay and free ;
And long may Beauty's dazzling power
   Reign over blooming Italy !

LOOK, MAIDEN, ON THESE LAUGHING FIELDS!

Look, maiden, on these laughing fields!
   But late they slept in winter's snow,
And now each opening blossom yields
   Rich fragrance, as the breezes blow.
What sing the birds ?—" it is the time
   When Pleasure woos our northern sky,
A moment woos, then quits a clime
   Too stern to hold her constantly !"

Forth let them speed ! who wish to wake,
   In summer shades, their woodland glee ;
For Autumn will his elf-locks shake,
   Ere many moons the young flowers see.
And, maiden of the snow-cold heart,
   Turn to thy life, perchance 'twill prove
Useful, to think how small a part,
   Is the glad season given to love.

OCH! WHILE I LIVE, I'LL NE'ER FORGET.

Och! while I live, I'll ne'er forget
   The troubles of that day,
When bound unto this distant land,
   Our ship got under weigh.
My friends I left at Belfast town,
   My love at Carrick shore,
And I gave to poor old Ireland
   My blessing o'er and o'er.

Och! well I knew, as off we sailed,
   What my hard fate would be;
For, gazing on my country's hills,
   They seemed to fly from me.
I watched them, as they wore away,
   Until my eyes grew sore,
And I felt that I was doomed to walk,
   The shamrock sod no more!

They say I'm now in Freedom's land,
  Where all men masters be ;
But were I in my winding-sheet,
  There's none to care for me !
I must, to eat the stranger's bread,
  Abide the stranger's scorn,
Who taunts me with thy dear-loved name,
  Sweet isle, where I was born !

Och ! where—och ! where's the careless heart
  I once could call my own ?
It bade a long farewell to me,
  The day I left Tyrone.
Not all the wealth, by hardship, won
  Beyond the western main,
Thy pleasures, my own absent home !
  Can bring to me again !

THE ARAB TO HIS HORSE.

THOU art fit for a son of Ismail !
  Thou art fit for the desert's own son !
Whose vengeance, so swift, strikes the morning all
      pale,
  At the deeds which the night hath seen done.
Fleeter far than the fleetest, the wind
  Would keep pace with thy shadow in vain ;
The scorching simoom thy light hoof cannot bind,
  When the caravans melt on the plain.

Through long ages, my fathers and thine
  Have controlled the dominions of sand ;
The tribute they claimed, at this moment, is mine,
  And my second thou art in command.
As the black-pinioned angel of Death
  Wings with fate his invisible spear,—

So thou, steed of pride ! urgest on, in his wrath,
    Thy dread lord when the foeman is near.

Alla loves us, my matchless Jereed !
    Thou dost joy in the feeling of might,
Which thrills through us both in the whirl of thy
        speed,
    When the moon can scarce follow our flight.
I shall still sweep the desert alone,
    Against me no power can prevail ;
The bare blade my sceptre, the saddle my throne,
    As becomes a true son of Ismail !

IT SPEAKS TO MY SPIRIT.

It speaks to my spirit the Voice of the Past,
  As I listlessly move on my way;
And pleasures, that were far too pleasant to last,
  Shine again, as they did in their day.
In an isle of the West, there's a tangled retreat,
  Which the sweet sun looks bashfully on,
And my soul has flown thither, in secret to meet
  With the feelings of years that are gone.

Across the broad meadow, and down the green lane,
  I have sped on the light foot of love,
And I stand, as I stood long ago, once again,
  By the old mossy seat in the grove.
Ah! yonder's the oak-tree, and under its shade
  One with looks full of welcome, I see;
Yes—yes—'tis my Ellen, in beauty arrayed,
  As she was, when she first met with me.

Remembrance is rapture—nay, smile if you please,
    While you point to my thin locks of gray,
Yet think not a heart, with emotions like these,
    Ever knows what it is to decay.
The furrow lies deep in my time-stricken cheek,
    And the life-blood rolls languidly on,
But the Voice of the Past has not yet ceased to speak
    With the feelings of years that are gone.

I DEARLY LOVED A GARDEN-FLOWER

I DEARLY loved a garden-flower
   Which near my summer casement grew;
Of all, that dwell in field or bower,
   None half so sweet I ever knew!
Many a time, with fond delight,
   I've bent its faultless form above,
And kissed its leaves, and deemed it might
   Still bloom for me, and be my love.

The autumn winds blew high, and bore
   My fairest from my sight away ;
I mourned its fate an hour or more,
   Then gave my heart to other sway.
A bird, with an enchanting note,
   The minstrel of an orange grove,
Became my captive, and I thought
   He'd live and share a maiden's love.

But one night, to my window, came
 The tinkle of a soft guitar,
And tones that hung upon my name—
 My bird's notes were less pleasant far !
I gave the warbler leave to go,
 In freedom, to his native grove,
And sighed, " Poor thing ! ah ! now I know,
 Thou wer't not meant to be my love !"

SONG OF THE SWITZER.

ABOVE are the Alps, and their snow,
Broad Leman reflects them below,
And O may its waters be blessed !
                    They span
The fields, by thy merry maids pressed,
                    Lausanne !

Long leagues of the shóre and the sea,
Divide my loved country from me ;
But Hope hath a sail and a steed
                    At hand,
That will bear me to thee with speed,
                    Sweet land !

We've toiled, and our labour is done ;
We've fought, and the battle is won ;

'Tis time that the soldier should cease
To roam,
'Tis time that he rest him in peace
At home.

O soon for the Alps, and their snow,
Shall the step of the war-exile go !
Where joy, in the years that are o'er,
Began,
His spirit shall bless thee once more,
Lausanne !

OLIVER & BOYD, PRINTERS.

Check Out More Titles From HardPress Classics Series In this collection we are offering thousands of classic and hard to find books. This series spans a vast array of subjects – so you are bound to find something of interest to enjoy reading and learning about.

Subjects:
Architecture
Art
Biography & Autobiography
Body, Mind &Spirit
Children & Young Adult
Dramas
Education
Fiction
History
Language Arts & Disciplines
Law
Literary Collections
Music
Poetry
Psychology
Science
…and many more.

Visit us at www.hardpress.net

Im TheStory
personalised classic books

JANE
IN
WONDERLAND

LEWIS
CARROLL

"Beautiful gift.. lovely finish,
My Niece loves it, so precious!"

Helen R Brumfieldon

★★★★★

UNIQUE
GIFT

FOR KIDS, PARTNERS
AND FRIENDS

Timeless books such as:

Kids

Alice in Wonderland · The Jungle Book · The Wonderful Wizard of Oz
Peter and Wendy · Robin Hood · The Prince and The Pauper
The Railway Children · Treasure Island · A Christmas Carol

Adults

Romeo and Juliet · Dracula

Highly
Customizable

Change
Books Title

Replace
Characters Names
with yours

Upload
Imagine that
inside page

Add
Inscriptions

Visit
Im TheStory.com
and order yours today!

CPSIA information can be obtained
at www.ICGtesting.com
Printed in the USA
BVHW041811220819
556561BV00022B/5535/P